NOT IF, BUT WHEN

†HE
APPEARiNG

SHAWN BOONSTRA

It Is Written
INTERNATION...

and Pacific Press Publishi...

Book Design & Layout by Fred Knopper
Cover Design by Palmer Halvorson
Illustrations by Palmer Halvorson and Steve Creitz
Edited by Judy Knopper

Additional copies of this book are available by
calling toll free 1-888-664-5573 or visiting
www.itiswritten.com

Printed in the United States of America
by Pacific Press Publishing Association
Nampa, Idaho / Oshawa, Ontario, Canada
www.pacificpress.com

ISBN: 0-8163-2116-7

Contents

Many thanks to Jean and the kids, who spent so
much time tiptoeing around the house
so that I could write.
I love you.

PREFACE

Once in a while, as I'm digging through a pile of books at a yard sale or flea market, I come across something by a famous author that was written before he or she became widely read or known. The book is usually well written (after all, *something* whetted the public's appetite for more books), but often does not reflect the maturity and well roundedness that belong to the author later in life.

Do authors cringe when they review what they have written? One of the unfortunate things about print media is that once a book has been published, your ideas have been forever cast in concrete. No matter how your understanding of the subject may mature in coming years, or how God leads you into experiences that may alter your perspective, your words cannot easily be retracted. When you discover a flaw, you can't run all over the country to gather up the copies you have already distributed. Subsequent editions and revisions (should you be so fortunate as to print them) may never find their way into the hands of those who read your first attempt.

I suspect that in years to come, if Jesus doesn't come first, I will one day open this book and shudder at the way I have presented this material.

I am also painfully aware, as I attempt to put thoughts on paper, that the depth of this subject is so profound that no human pen (or word processor) could possibly hope to do it justice. The subject is Jesus Christ and is therefore infinite.

As I begin to write, the words that John used to close his gospel come to mind: "And there are also many other things that Jesus did, which if they were written one by one, I suppose that even the world itself could not contain the books that would be written" (John 21:25).

John knew there was more to the story than the words he had written. If a divinely inspired biographer felt that way as he finished his work, imagine how I feel as I place this book in your hands. John had first-hand knowledge of Christ's life. His thoughts were directed by the power of the Holy Spirit. His book was literally *breathed by God*, and yet he knew that what he had written was only the tip of the iceberg. Anything *I* write about Jesus will be woefully inadequate, unless God takes a coal from the heavenly altar and touches it to my lips—or in this case, my laptop.

There is just one more word of caution as you begin reading the pages that follow. The subject of this book is the Second Coming of Christ. In his letter to Titus, Paul called Christ's return "the blessed hope," and with good reason. For centuries, Christians have clung to the hope that Jesus will return. The thought of His coming sustains us through life's toughest times. It buoys us up when hope seems slim. It unites us as Christians—and yet few subjects have proven to be such fertile ground for heated debate among Christians.

I have seen Christians storm out of church because they didn't like the preacher's take on last-day events. I have witnessed well-meaning Christians disown one another's faith because of differing viewpoints on Bible prophecy.

This is not appropriate behavior for Christians. Anyone who believes that they have nothing to learn will arrest their spiritual development. Even such luminaries as John the Baptist and the disciples misunderstood prophecy at times. This obviously did not disqualify them as Christians or separate them from the body of Christ.

It is entirely possible that as you read the pages that follow you will come across something that does not resonate with what you have always understood or believed. That's OK. Just be sure that you appeal to the scriptures alone for what you will believe. Search the Bible carefully. In this late hour before Jesus comes, Christians need to set aside their philosophical and religious differences to ask just one question: what does *God* say?

It's amazing how clearly God can speak for Himself if we'd just let Him.

March 2005

INTRODUCTION

It was Shrove Tuesday, 1945. The night air was clear over the city of Dresden, Germany. Children had already gone to bed. Shadows danced on the walls of thousands of homes as families waited out the last moments of the day gathered around their fireplaces. Some shared stories. Others silently wondered when their loved ones would be returning from the battlefields of Europe.

Suddenly, at about 9:30 P.M., the mournful wail of air-raid sirens filled the air. Everyone stopped cold. *Could it really be?* Nobody seriously expected Dresden to be a target. Of course, it was always possible, but few people believed it could actually happen. Hearts stopped cold. Anxious parents quickly glanced at each other. Mothers ran to grab their children. Maybe it would be just another false alarm.

All over the city trembling fingers grappled with radio dials. A frenzied announcer confirmed their worst fears. The planes were really coming. Dresden was under attack.

Families scrambled to remember inadequately rehearsed emergency plans. There was no use trying to find an air-raid shelter in the city; they were already packed to capacity with refugees from the eastern front. Those who had access to cellars or basements quickly disappeared into them. Many would never resurface.

Moments later the bloodcurdling drone of Allied bombers enveloped the city, followed by what seemed like endless explosions that shook the earth violently. The city began to burn, and the intense heat rose so quickly into the night air that it created a powerful vacuum that uprooted trees and sucked those unfortunate enough to be outdoors into the flames.

The pounding was merciless, continuing through the night and well into the next day. Endless waves of Allied planes dropped their lethal loads on the helpless citizens of Dresden. It was one of the worst calamities of the Second World War. Estimates of the death toll range from 35,000-100,000 people. When it was over, a once-beautiful medieval city lay in smoldering ruins.

According to the words of Jesus, His return to this world will creep up on millions of people like a "thief in the night." Many who hear the trumpet blast will be caught by surprise. It's not that they didn't know about the *possibility* of Christ's coming; it's just that they didn't really expect it to happen.

The bombing of Dresden is a sober lesson in lack of preparedness. Historians have guessed that most people in the city didn't really think it could happen, in spite of the fact that there was a devastating war raging all over the continent. Many people had developed a tragically false sense of security, and a lack of preparedness cost thousands of people their lives.

The Bible predicts that, in the final moments before Christ returns, there will be those who scoff at the idea:

Knowing this first: that scoffers will come in the last days, walking according to their own lusts, and saying, "Where is the promise of His coming? For since the fathers fell asleep, all things continue as they were from the beginning of creation. (2 Peter 3:3, 4)

A few years ago, in the middle of a conversation, an acquaintance of mine suddenly blurted out, "All this talk about the end of the world, and it still hasn't happened! People have thought that Jesus would come for hundreds of years now, and He hasn't, has He?"

I was surprised by the outburst since the topic at hand had nothing to do with religion, let alone the Second Coming. This woman was not an atheist; in fact, she has attended church all her life—and yet she does not believe in the Second Coming of Christ. Years ago, I used to think Peter was talking about so-called "worldly people" when he spoke of last-day scoffers, but I've changed my mind. A lot of the scoffing seems to be taking place in the church.

Tragically, for those who choose to disbelieve, the appearance of Christ will come as a devastating surprise. It will be like Shrove Tuesday in Dresden:

But the day of the Lord will come as a thief in the night, in which the heavens will pass away with a great noise, and the elements will melt with fervent heat; both the earth and the works that are in it will be burned up. (2 Peter 3:10)

The parallels are sobering. In the city of Dresden, people were well aware that there was a war being raged all around them. In our world today, there are few people who do not sense that there is a massive spiritual struggle between good and evil taking place. With the passing of time, however, many people have been lulled into complacency. They simply assume Christ's appearing will never happen, at least not in their lifetime.

Given the sterling track record of Bible prophecy, which in thousands of years has never been wrong, I'm convinced it *will* happen. The big question, of course, is *when?*

A story from the Dresden bombing will begin to answer the question. After the loss of human life, one of the worst tragedies of this incident was the destruction of priceless antique documents in the city library. At the time, the library housed one of the most important South American documents in existence—an ancient manuscript known as the Dresden Codex. Anxious curators ran to the library to find out if it had survived. To their great relief, apart from being a little singed along the edges, it was fine.

What was so important about this document? The Dresden Codex is one of three ancient Mayan books that somehow managed to survive a series of misguided book-burnings conducted by Spanish clergymen in South America in the early 1500s. Of the three surviving manuscripts, the Dresden Codex is the best preserved, and perhaps the most useful to historians. It provides us with an amazing glimpse of ancient Mayan culture and beliefs. It is something like a Mayan Rosetta Stone that unlocks the mysteries of a long-lost civilization.

The book has more than 70 pages. Rather than being bound like a modern volume, its form is a long piece of tree-bark paper that is folded up like an accordion. The content of the manuscript is remarkable:

The codex was written by eight different scribes, each with their own distinctive style, type of glyphs and subject matter. It is linked to the Yucatecan Maya in Chichén Itzá, the extraordinary ancient Mayan city situated in the north of the Yucatán Peninsula. It was made between A.D. 1200-1250, and was still possibly in use when the conquistadors arrived. The "Codex Dresdensis" as one of the few pre-Columbian Mayan hieroglyphic writings (most of them on stelas found in Palenque, one of the ancient cities of Yucatán) contains astronomical calculations of exceptional accuracy. There are almanacs and day counts for worship and prophecies; two astronomical and astrological tables, one dealing with eclipses and the other Venus and katún (a 20-year period) prophecies. It contains references and predictions for time and agriculture, favorable days for predictions, as well as texts about sickness, medicine, and seemingly, conjunctions of constellations, planets and the Moon. It also contains a page about a flood, a prophecy or maybe a reference to the rainy seasons so vital to the Maya.[1]

Like the ancient Babylonians, the Mayans were shrewd students of the heavens. Generations of Mayan scholars measured the paths of stars through the night sky, and produced astronomical measurements that continue to amaze modern scholars. Many of their astonishing observations are recorded in the Dresden Codex.

The Mayans viewed the world in terms of rhythmic historical cycles. Their calendar clearly reflects this belief. Placing the date of creation at about 3114 B.C. (by our calendar), they traced a number of repetitive cycles in nature, and using those cycles as checkpoints they made a number of predictions about the course of history. On December 21, 2012, the Mayan calendar abruptly ends. They believed it to be the end of the world.

In a world steeped in New Age philosophy, this ancient Mayan prophecy has generated a lot of wild speculation. A quick search of the Internet will show you just how widespread people's fascination with the year 2012 has become in recent years. Some people have tried to find this date laid out in the measurements of the Great Pyramid. Others have tried to tie it to the writings of Nostradamus, who also predicted that something cataclysmic would befall our planet after the year 2000. I've even heard the occasional Christian minister make reference to this date as if it were a sign that we are nearing the end.

Is there anything to it? Personally, I do not place any stock in the prediction. I do not believe that the ancient Mayans had a magical key to the future. Given the Mayan track record in other areas of spirituality, I cannot accept that they had a God-given gift of prophecy. The only reason that I've raised the subject at all is because in addition to generating a lot of modern speculation, the 2012 date points out something important: *the Mayans believed the world would end.*

That may not seem like rocket science to you, but ask yourself this question: why did they believe this? For that matter, why did so many ancient cultures also believe the world would end? The ancient Assyrians, Romans, and Zoroastrians, for example, all made apocalyptic predictions at some point. After assessing the state of the world, they concluded, along with modern-day Christianity, that the world is gradually degenerating, and will someday come to a grinding halt.

I do not believe that it is a mere coincidence that so many ancient cultures believed in a last day or final judgment. God has planted an uneasy sense in the human heart that something is wrong with our world. Instinctively, we know that something is amiss. In spite of our insistence that the human race is slowly evolving into something better, a small, still voice in our hearts tells us otherwise. We have a sense of uneasiness about where the world is heading.

In Ecclesiastes 3:11, we read that God has "put eternity in (our) hearts." Buried somewhere deep within the human heart is a desire for something better. We intuitively sense that pain and suffering are not the natural order of things. We feel sorrow when we suffer loss. We become angry when we witness unjust behavior. We complain when things aren't fair. Why?

The human race seems to have a collective memory of a time when things were better. Communists, sensing the injustice of the world we live in, tried to manufacture a political system that would eradicate inequality. The more radical members of the modern environmental movement try to return to "the way things were." Materialists try to better their station in life with possessions. Scientists try to manufacture solutions for human ailments in the laboratory.

Why do we do these things? Why do we assume that suffering is wrong? Why do we assume there's a possibility for improvement? Is it because God has planted a sense of eternity in our hearts?

All around the world, the human race is crying out for something better. Parents of starving children long to be able to feed them. Lonely people crave companionship. Those suffering the ravages of war, yearn for peace. A longing for home overwhelms us.

As we sit poised at the opening of a new millennium, there's a growing sense that it may no longer be business as usual on planet earth. Scores of ancient biblical prophecies about the return of Christ are coming to pass before our eyes. The planet's pulse is quickening. Could it really be? Are we the generation that will finally see it happen?

_____

[1]   http://www.tu-dresden.de/slub/proj/maya/mayaeng.html

CHAPTER ONE

The Keys of Death

Ancient stone steps led down into a cold, musty passageway scarcely wide enough for two people. Earthen walls and a growing sense of solemnity pressed in on us as we followed the kindly priest deeper and deeper into the earth under the Roman countryside. Dimly lit shelves carved into the sides of the tunnel marked the places where, eighteen centuries ago, grieving families had carefully laid the bodies of their loved ones. Timeworn etchings on the soft volcanic wall expressed sentiments we could scarcely read. We pressed on through countless somber corridors, until our guide suddenly stopped.

"Take a look in here," he said. In a big recess to the side of the tunnel, there was a large stone box cut out of the earth. It was about the size of a large chest freezer. A flood lamp mounted on the ceiling lit the inside of the box with an eerie glow. Cautiously, we leaned over and peered into the box. It was empty.

"This was a family grave," the priest explained, his eyes sparkling with the delight that comes from being excited about your subject. "The bodies of pagans were deposited by their families all over the countryside, but the early Christians wanted to be buried together. That's the whole point of these catacombs. The early church didn't believe that death was forever, so they wanted to sleep together until the resurrection."

They didn't believe that death was forever? Nearly two millennia have passed, and the thousands of Christians who are buried in the catacombs are still dead. How could anyone seriously believe in life after death? Yet that's precisely what Christians continue to believe almost two thousand years later.

Ancient pagans referred to a place of burial as a *necropolis*, or "city of the dead." To their way of thinking, nobody ever came back from a necropolis, except maybe to haunt the living as a disembodied spirit. Early Christians, on the other hand, referred to the graveyard as a *cemetery*, which is really an ancient Greek word (*koimeterion*) that means *dormitory*. It was a place where people slept. They would not be dead forever, because one day, heaven's alarm clock would ring, Christ would return, and the dead would wake up.

Why did they believe that? The early Christians were not naïve simpletons who believed in the possibility of resurrection because they didn't really understand death. In reality they lived much closer to the subject than we do. Our twenty-first century North American experience usually consists of hospital waiting rooms, silk-lined caskets and funeral homes. As difficult as those things are, they pale by comparison with the early Christian experience. Our forefathers saw their friends beheaded, torn apart by wild animals, or burned alive and used to light the Roman games at night.

Their understanding of death was quite real, and yet they believed that the dead would live again. What possible reason could they have for this hope? The answer is staggering: *they already knew of someone who had come back from the grave.*

The Christian church makes an astonishing claim. The founder of their faith has come back from the dead. Writing to the Christian believers in Corinth, the apostle Paul said:

For I delivered to you first of all that which I also received: that Christ died for our sins according to the Scriptures, and that He was buried, and that He rose again the third day according to the Scriptures, and that He was seen by Cephas, then by the twelve. After that He was seen by over five hundred brethren at once, of whom the greater part remain to the present, but some have fallen asleep. After that He was seen by James, then by all the apostles. Then last of all He was seen by me also, as by one born out of due time. (1 Corinthians 15:3-8)

Hundreds of early Christian believers saw Jesus after His resurrection. They knew for a fact that He was alive. They were so convinced of it that they were willing to stake their own lives on it. All but one of the apostles died a martyr's death. Andrew and Philip were crucified. Peter was crucified upside-down because he insisted that to be crucified like Jesus was too good for him. Matthias was stoned and then beheaded. James was bludgeoned to death after being pushed off the temple. Mark was dragged to death.

They were willing to put their lives on the line for Christ because they knew, firsthand, what Jesus had accomplished at the cross. They knew that He had defeated death. All of them insisted, to the very end, that Jesus was alive—and that He would return for them.

Christ Himself had told the disciples that He had a plan to return to this world:

"Let not your heart be troubled; you believe in God, believe also in Me. In My Father's house are many mansions; if it were not so, I would have told you. I go to prepare a place for you. And if I go and prepare a place for you, I will come again and receive you to Myself; that where I am, there you may be also." (John 14:1-3)

The disciples believed, in their hearts, that when Jesus came back, He would reverse the tragedy of the grave and bring the dead back to life:

But now Christ is risen from the dead, and has become the firstfruits of those who have fallen asleep. For since by man came death, by Man also came the resurrection of the dead. For as in Adam all die, even so in Christ all shall be made alive. But each one in his own order: Christ the firstfruits, afterward those who are Christ's at His coming. Then comes the end, when He delivers the kingdom to God the Father, when He puts an end to all rule and all authority and power. For He must reign till He has put all enemies under His feet. The last enemy that will be destroyed is death. (1 Corinthians 15:20-26)

But I do not want you to be ignorant, brethren, concerning those who have fallen asleep, lest you sorrow as others who have no hope. For if we believe that Jesus died and rose again, even so God will bring with Him those who sleep in Jesus. For this we say to you by the word of the Lord, that we who are alive and remain until the coming of the Lord will by no means precede those who are asleep. For the Lord Himself shall descend from heaven with a shout, with the voice of an archangel, and with the trumpet of God. And the dead in Christ will rise first. Then we who are alive and remain shall be caught up together with them in the clouds to meet the Lord in the air. And thus we shall always be with the Lord. Therefore comfort one another with these words. (1 Thessalonians 4:13-18)

No wonder the early Christians referred to their burial chambers as dormitories! A dormitory is not hopeless. You don't spend eternity there; you merely spend the night. Sleep is a temporary condition.

Admittedly, the night has been a long one. As I stood in the ancient Roman tunnels beside my wife, I was painfully aware that those tunnels were eighteen hundred years old. For almost two thousand years, Christians have read the ancient prophecies and looked up into the sky, wondering when it will happen. Generation after generation has been laid to sleep, and Christ has still not come.

Were the early Christians wrong? Or is there evidence in the Bible to suggest that we were *supposed* to expect a delay?

I have heard many people suggest that the early Christians expected the Second Coming at any moment, and to some extent, this is true. The Bible record indicates that, at one point, the church in Thessalonica believed that Jesus would return in their lifetime. Paul's first letter to that church, which contains one of the passages quoted above, apparently gave them the idea that it was already time for Jesus to return. In his second letter, he sets the record straight:

Now, brethren, concerning the coming of our Lord Jesus Christ and our gathering together to Him, we ask you, not to be soon shaken in mind or troubled, either by spirit or by word or by letter, as if from us, as though the day of Christ had come. Let no one deceive you by any means, for that Day will not come unless the falling away comes first.... (2 Thessalonians 2:1-3a)

"Don't get too worked up," Paul tells them, "because it's not time for Jesus to come yet. There are some things that have to happen first."

There is further evidence to suggest that there would be a delay. In Peter's second letter, he tells us that enough time would pass for people to start mocking the idea of a Second Coming:

...knowing this first: that scoffers will come in the last days, walking according to their own lusts, and saying, "Where is the promise of His coming? For since the fathers fell asleep, all things continue as they were from the beginning of creation." (2 Peter 3:3, 4)

Later in that same passage, Peter offers us a reminder that it might seem like an eternity until Jesus returns. Enough time will pass that people will begin to doubt. We might be tempted to think that God is slack in keeping His promises. To help us avoid that temptation, Peter writes:

But, beloved, do not forget this one thing, that with the Lord one day is as a thousand years, and a thousand years as one day. The Lord is not slack concerning His promise.... (2 Peter 3:8, 9)

Jesus Himself predicted that there would be a perceived delay in His return. He compared the believers to a group of women waiting for a bridegroom to arrive, and said, "But while the bridegroom was delayed, they all slumbered and slept" (Matthew 25:5).

What's interesting about this passage is the fact that Jesus is speaking about members of His church. These are people who were *expecting* Christ to come, and experienced a delay. Sadly, instead of keeping vigil, they fell asleep. They assumed there was time to rest. They were wrong:

And at midnight a cry was heard: "Behold, the bridegroom is coming; go out to meet Him!" (Matthew 25:6).

At some point, we will finally be roused out of slumber by the sound of Christ's return. A loud cry will call our planet to get ready for Jesus to come. More than two thousand ancient biblical prophecies tell us to expect the return of Jesus Christ. Scores of inspired prophets saw it happen in vision. Over the centuries, millions have waited for it, clinging to hope against all odds. Those who were laid to rest in the Roman catacombs drew their last breath anticipating it. They knew they were going to wake up.

Eventually, some generation is going to witness it. As the pulse of the planet quickens, and countless visions of ancient prophets become modern headlines, there are growing indications that *we might be that generation.*

CHAPTER TWO

History Written in Advance

He woke up suddenly, in the middle of the night. His heart was pounding; beads of cold sweat ran off of his forehead into some of the most luxurious pillows money could buy. Was it real, or had he just dreamed it? What did it mean?

He tried to go back to sleep, but it was of no use, because he couldn't shake the sense of fear coursing through his veins. He swung himself out of bed and stood up, his heart still thumping wildly in his chest. It took him a moment to get his bearings, and then he marched out of the room. His servants, posted outside the door, snapped to attention.

"Call everyone together," he barked. "I want the Chaldeans, the astrologers, the sorcerers, and the magicians."

They scrambled to make his command a reality. When the king of Babylon wants something, you make it happen. Moments later, everyone was gathered in the presence of the sleep-deprived ruler. What was so important that it demanded a meeting in the middle of the night? The king looked over the group and chose his words very deliberately.

"I've had a dream, and I'm anxious to know what it means...."

History tells us that the ancients lived in awe of their dreams. When a dream was particularly vivid, it was considered to be a message from the gods. According to one source, the most common subject matter of ancient Egyptian dreams included:

- Breaking stones
- Drowning in the Nile
- Having your face turn into a leopard's
- Drinking warm beer
- Eating white bread
- Having your teeth fall out

When we have this sort of dream, we tend to laugh it off. Our ancient forefathers *never* laughed off a memorable dream. If you couldn't shake the memory of a haunting night vision, the gods *must* be trying to tell you something important.

Roughly 2600 years ago, the king of Babylon had one such disturbing dream, the content of which literally shaped the course of world history. Nebuchadnezzar's memorable night is recorded in the second chapter of the book of Daniel:

Now in the second year of Nebuchadnezzar's reign, Nebuchadnezzar had dreams; and his spirit was so troubled that his sleep left him. Then the king gave the command to call the magicians, the astrologers, the sorcerers, and the Chaldeans to tell the king his dreams. So they came and stood before the king. And the king said to them, "I have had a dream, and my spirit is anxious to know the dream." Then the Chaldeans spoke to the king in Aramaic, "O king, live forever! Tell your servants the dream, and we will give you the interpretation." (Daniel 2:1-4)

The content of the dream was so disturbing that the king couldn't fall back asleep. After tossing and turning for a while, he called the wisest men of the realm together to help him understand what was happening. They were all too happy to comply. "Just tell us what you dreamed, and we'll tell you what it means," they assured him. In a few moments, they assumed, everyone would be safely tucked back in bed and the whole incident would be over.

"Not so fast," the king said. "First, I want you to tell me what I dreamed."

But the king answered and said to the Chaldeans, "My decision is firm: if you do not make known the dream to me, and its interpretation, you shall be cut in pieces, and your houses shall be made an ash heap." (Daniel 2:5)

Students of the Bible differ on what actually happened at this point. Some believe that Nebuchadnezzar couldn't remember the dream; others believe that he was just testing the Chaldeans, who claimed to be able to hear from the gods. One thing is certain: Nebuchadnezzar knew his dream was of utmost importance. He was right. Not only did it signal important events for his kingdom, it also painted a vivid panorama of world history, right down to its startling. He was anxious to know what it meant, so he threatened his counselors that unless they revealed the content of the dream and explained it, they would lose their lives.

He should have suspected what would happen. The Chaldeans simply couldn't deliver. It was beyond their realm of expertise to get inside the king's head and extract the dream. "There is not a man on earth who can tell the king's matter," they said, "therefore no king, lord, or ruler has ever asked such things of any magician, astrologer, or Chaldean. It is a difficult thing that the king requires, and there is no other who can tell it to the king except the gods, whose dwelling is not with flesh." (Daniel 2:10, 11)

These men were probably telling Nebuchadnezzar the truth for the first time in their lives. Like many modern soothsayers and psychics, they had made a career out of pretending to have a connection with the spirit realm, but all the while they were spinning pleasing stories for the king. This night, their sins caught up with them. They failed miserably.

The king was beside himself. His temper erupted. He gave the order to destroy all the wise men of Babylon. The search began immediately. Among those being sought was a young Hebrew captive named Daniel.

Then with counsel and wisdom Daniel answered Arioch, the captain of the king's guard, who had gone out to kill the wise men of Babylon; he answered and said to Arioch the king's captain, "Why is the decree from the king so urgent?" Then Arioch made the decision known to Daniel. So Daniel went in and asked the king to give him time, that he might tell the king the interpretation. (Daniel 2:14-16)

There was something about Daniel that soothed the king's nerves. When the Chaldeans had asked for more time, it had infuriated him. He knew they were stalling because they couldn't produce the dream. Daniel was different. He seemed to have a genuine link to heaven. In the past, he had proven himself as an interpreter of dreams and visions (Daniel 1: 17). The extra time that Daniel requested was granted.

Daniel hurried back to his friends, and they spent the night in prayer. They didn't resort to star charts, crystal balls or tealeaves. On their knees, they stepped into the throne room of heaven, and brought their request to God. Their prayer was answered:

Then the secret was revealed in a night vision. So Daniel blessed the God of heaven. (Daniel 2:19,20)

In the morning, Daniel raced over to see Arioch, the man assigned to destroy the wise men of Babylon. "Don't kill anyone," he said, "because I have it! Take me to the king, and I'll tell him all about his dream."

It may have happened 2600 years ago, but what happens next in this ancient story has a direct bearing on the twenty-first century. As Daniel steps into the presence of the king, he pulls back the curtains of the universe and allows us a brief glance at God's divine timetable for planet earth:

"You, O king, were watching; and behold, a great image! This great image, whose splendor was excellent, stood before you; and its form was awesome. This image's head was of fine gold, its chest and arms of silver, its belly and thighs of bronze, its legs of iron, its feet partly of iron and partly of clay. You watched while a stone was cut out without hands, which struck the image on its feet of iron and clay, and broke them in pieces. Then the iron, the clay, the bronze, the silver, and the gold were crushed together, and became like chaff from the summer threshing floors; the wind carried them away so that no trace of them was found. And the stone that struck the image became a great mountain and filled the whole earth." (Daniel 2:31-35)

Statues were commonplace in ancient Babylon. They were an important part of everyday religion and life—but whereas most of them were made of solid gold (or some other single material), the statue in the king's dream was different. It was a composite. It had a golden head, a silver chest, a bronze (or brass, in some translations) belly and thighs, iron legs, and feet made of a mixture of iron and clay. As Nebuchadnezzar was looking at it, a large stone suddenly flew out of nowhere and smashed the statue to bits. The wind blew away the pieces, and the stone grew until it filled the earth.

It was hardly the stuff of nightmares, yet something about it troubled the king profoundly. Sometimes a dream will cause you a great deal of discomfort in spite of the fact that the content itself is not all that terrifying.

This dream was enough to rob the king of sleep. The interpretation of the dream should shake us out of *our* complacency, too—because it has something important to say about Christ's return.

Daniel Explains the Dream

Imagine meeting someone who could tell you what you dreamed last night. Impossible, right? No wonder Daniel had the king's undivided attention:

"This is the dream. Now we will tell the interpretation of it before the king. You, O king, are a king of kings. For the God of heaven has given you a kingdom, power, strength, and glory; and wherever the children of men dwell, or the beasts of the field and the birds of the heaven, He has given them into your hand, and has made you ruler over them all—you are this head of gold." (Daniel 2:36-38)

There is no mistaking the meaning of Nebuchadnezzar's dream. It is not open for debate, because the Bible tells us quite plainly what it means. The head of gold, perched on top of the statue, represents the Babylonian empire of Nebuchadnezzar. The king must have been very pleased with this interpretation; gold was the most valuable metal in the vision, and the head was obviously the most important part of the statue.

Daniel's words, incidentally, were not mere flattery. The empire that God had allowed Nebuchadnezzar to build was both very extensive and fabulously wealthy. Many years later, when the historian Herodotus visited the city, he gave a report of its wealth that almost defies imagination:

> In the temple of Babylon there is a second shrine lower down, in which is a great sitting figure of Bel, all of gold on a golden throne, supported on a base of gold, with a golden table standing beside it. I was told by the Chaldeans that, to make all this, more than twenty-two tons of gold were used.[2]

It took twenty-two tons of gold just to furnish the *secondary* shrine of the temple! Babylon's wealth is hard for modern minds to grasp. Her citizens enjoyed every conceivable comfort in life, and the very name of the city became a symbol of decadence for generations to come. Even to this day, people still speak of "Babylon" in reference to unbridled self-indulgence.

As Daniel spoke to the king, however, the sun was setting on the great Babylonian empire. The hands of heaven's clock were approaching midnight and the kingdom was about to collapse. Nebuchadnezzar's grandson, Belshazzar, would be the last member of the royal family to occupy the throne:

"But after you shall arise another kingdom inferior to yours; then another, a third kingdom of bronze, which shall rule over all the earth. And the fourth kingdom shall be as strong as iron, inasmuch as iron breaks in pieces and shatters all things; and like iron that crushes, that kingdom will break in pieces and crush all the others." (Daniel 2:39, 40)

"After your kingdom falls," Daniel explains, "there will be three more empires."

Heaven, of course, is always right. Babylon collapsed in 539 B.C. when Cyrus the Persian diverted the mighty Euphrates River, which ran through Babylon, at some distance north of the city. The water level dropped to thigh-deep near the city wall, thus creating a virtual highway under the wall. The only obstacle the Persians faced once they followed the riverbed into the city was a pair of walls with heavily guarded gates that lined the length of the river. If they could not manage to find a quick way through the gates, they would be sitting ducks for the Babylonian army.

An Unseen Hand was on the side of the Persians. On the night they entered the city, Nebuchadnezzar's grandson Belshazzar was in the middle of a massive citywide drunken feast. The gates along the river were recklessly left unattended and unlocked. Babylon fell quickly.

Perhaps one of the most amazing things about the collapse of Babylon is the fact that the prophet Isaiah predicted it in stunning detail more than 100 years before Cyrus was born:

Who says to the deep, "Be dry! And I will dry up your rivers"; Who says of Cyrus, "He is My shepherd, And he shall perform all My pleasure, Even saying to Jerusalem, You shall be built," and to the temple, "Your foundation shall be laid."

Thus says the Lord to His anointed, To Cyrus, whose right hand I have held—to subdue nations before him and loose the armor of kings, to open before him the double doors, so that the gates will not be shut; "I will go before you and make the crooked places straight; I will break in pieces the gates of bronze and cut the bars of iron." (Isaiah 44:27-45:2)

One of the strongest arguments in favor of trusting Bible prophecy is the fact that it has never once been wrong. How in the world did Isaiah predict Cyrus by name before he was born? And how did he get all the details right so many years in advance—from the drying of the river to the open gates inside the city—unless guided by the divine hand of God?

The Medo-Persian empire (a coalition government between the Medes and the Persians) governed the known world for a couple of centuries, but then it also collapsed. In 331 B.C., the Macedonians under Alexander the Great defeated the Persians against all odds at the battle of Arbela. With amazing swiftness, Alexander marched over 20,000 miles and never lost a single battle. He managed to unite 22 million square miles of empire under his control. The Greek language became the language of commerce and learning for centuries to come—which is the reason that our New Testament was written in Greek.

As impressive as Alexander's accomplishments were, he never managed to conquer his own passions. When his armies reached the east coast of India, legend tells us that he assumed there were no more worlds to conquer and he wept. On his way back home, he stopped in the city of Babylon, where it is believed that he died as a result of alcohol consumption.

After Alexander's death, there was a brief power struggle, and eventually, the empire was divided into four parts under four of his generals. In 168 B.C., the Greek empire was finally dismantled by the Romans—the empire which ruled the world when Christ was born.

We know the history of world empires because we are able to extract details from meticulous records handed down by ancient historians. *Daniel knew world history before it happened.*

What happens next is even more amazing. Someone could argue that the four empires were a lucky guess, but what Daniel predicted next, no one could have possibly guessed. It seals his status as a genuine prophet of God. After the fourth empire, the story changes a little:

"Whereas you saw the feet and toes, partly of potter's clay and partly of iron, the kingdom shall be divided; yet the strength of the iron shall be in it, just as you saw the iron mixed with ceramic clay. And as the toes of the feet were partly of iron and partly of clay, so the kingdom shall be partly strong and partly fragile. As you saw iron mixed with ceramic clay, they will mingle with the seed of men; but they will not adhere to one another, just as iron does not mix with clay." (Daniel 2:41-43)

There would not be a fifth empire. Exactly as God had revealed to Nebuchadnezzar, the Western Roman Empire crumbled as barbarian tribes from Europe repeatedly laid siege to it. When it finally collapsed in 476 A.D., it was *not* succeeded by another world empire. It broke into ten pieces—just as the statue had ten toes.[3] Over the next 1500 years, seven of the ten fragments evolved into the modern nations of Western Europe.[4]

The precision of this prophecy is breathtaking. It covers more than 2,000 years of history. What's more, Daniel prophesied that the pieces of the Roman empire would never be put back together. "They will mingle with the seed of men, but they will not adhere to one another," he said.

What does this mean? For generations, kings, generals and diplomats have tried to piece together the Roman Empire—"mingling the seed of men"—but each attempt has ended in abysmal failure. The pieces simply won't stick together.

Some tried to reunite the empire through political alliances and strategic intermarriage. By the time Queen Victoria was in the latter years of her reign, she was nicknamed "the Grandmother of Europe." This was because she was literally related to many of the heads of state across the continent. Both her children and grandchildren married into a number of Europe's royal families. Among her grandchildren were the German Emperor Wilhelm II; Maud, the queen consort of Norway; Alexandra of Russia; Queen Sophie of Greece; Marie, consort to King Ferdinand of Romania; and Queen Victoria Eugenie of Spain.[5]

Many of the royal marriages of Europe were a matter of convenience rather than love. Couples were united because alliances between nations were being forged—yet these alliances utterly failed to reunite the nations of Western Europe under one head of state. Historians have tried to speculate why European unity has been so elusive. Yet an ancient pagan king knew the truth: the Western Roman Empire cannot be reunited because *God said it would not be*.

At this very moment, influential politicians in Europe are working feverishly to cement the future of the European Union. To some degree, they've been successful. Twenty-five years ago, when I visited family in Europe, I had to present a passport at every border crossing. Now, when you enter Europe, you only need to show your passport at the first country you enter. After that, the borders are wide open. It's almost as if the western half of the continent is all one nation. Interestingly, there are distinct challenges to the European Economic Community. Although a balanced budget is a condition of membership, a number of member nations have consistently presented a deficit budget. And, at the time of this writing, England refuses to adopt the Euro as its unit of currency. The question of involvement in the war in Iraq drew deep political lines all across the union. Every time unity appears within grasp, something seems to happen to move it just out of reach.

Even if the European Economic Community manages to establish a reasonable degree of unity, an economic free trade zone is still not the same as political unity. There will not be a restoration of the Roman Empire.

The history of Western Europe stands as a powerful testimony to the truth of Nebuchadnezzar's dream. Charlemagne attempted to unite the empire but utterly failed. Charles V, elected Holy Roman Emperor in 1519, tried his best, but the spread of the Protestant Reformation in Germany suddenly prevented European unity. The wars of Spanish succession demolished the dreams of Louis XIV of France. Napoleon, as fiercely successful as he was, found himself powerless against the Russian winter and hopelessly outmaneuvered at Waterloo.

Why did these men fail? It certainly wasn't because they weren't capable of pulling it off. It had more to do with the fact that God said it was impossible.

The twentieth century was no different. Woodrow Wilson campaigned for the American presidency in 1916 on the promise that he would keep his nation out of the battlefields of World War One, and that's exactly what Germany wanted. The Kaiser was within striking distance of winning the war if he could only keep America from getting involved.

The British were desperate to enlist American help in their efforts to fight the Kaiser, but to no avail—that is, until early in 1917. A German diplomat by the name of Arthur Zimmerman sent an encrypted telegram to Mexico, encouraging an alliance between the two nations. He tried to persuade the Mexicans to cause trouble on the Mexican-American border, which would keep the United States busy enough on the home front to prevent them from developing an interest in the war.

By some miracle, the British managed to intercept the telegram. Personally, I'm convinced that God wanted them to have it. After decoding the message, they sent a copy to the American government. Enraged by Germany's desire to cause trouble for America, they got involved in the war. In the end, the Kaiser lost.

A young soldier in the Kaiser's army was humiliated by the defeat and developed a strong desire to restore Germany's pride. His name was Adolph Hitler, and he swore that he would succeed where Napoleon had failed. He would build an empire that would last a thousand years.

Hitler's Third Reich led to the Second World War. By 1941, the future looked pretty rosy for Germany, but in the end, after a devastating turn of events, Hitler took his own life while hiding in a bunker.

Why did Hitler lose? Historians can point to a number of factors that certainly had something to do with it, but the number one reason had more to do with an ancient king's dream than with military strategy or modern political affairs: *God has irrevocably declared that it will be impossible to reunite the Western Roman Empire.*

Peering down the corridors of time, Nebuchadnezzar saw our day. He saw the nations that would sprout from the collapsed Roman Empire. He saw the world we live in at this very moment. And perhaps the most sobering thing about the prophecy is that the *ten toes are the final chapter of the story:*

"And in the days of these kings the God of heaven will set up a kingdom which shall never be destroyed; and the kingdom shall not be left to other people; it shall break in pieces and consume all these kingdoms, and it shall stand forever." (Daniel 2:44)

There will not be another global human empire. There may be last-day global deceptions and religious movements, but there will not be another global political empire. God Himself will set up the next kingdom.

How does God establish a kingdom? At some point, in the courts of heaven, a kingdom is given to Jesus Christ:

"I was watching in the night visions, and behold, One like the Son of Man, coming with the clouds of heaven! He came to the Ancient of Days, and they brought Him near before Him. Then to Him was given dominion and glory and a kingdom, that all peoples, nations and languages should serve Him. His dominion is an everlasting dominion, which shall not pass away, and His kingdom the one which shall not be destroyed." (Daniel 7:13, 14)

Human beings do not establish Christ's kingdom; God Himself establishes it. That's why Daniel was able to say that the stone that crushed the image was "cut out without hands." It will not be built on human political intrigue or by those who stuff ballot boxes to corrupt an election. It will not be established in the midst of a bloody civil war or by a *coup d'etat*. Rather, it will be handed to Christ by the Ancient of Days.

There is a line drawn in the sands of time that God will not allow the human race to cross. In full view of millions of heavenly angels, human government will have had enough time to clearly demonstrate that human beings are ultimately incapable of governing themselves. Centuries of heartache, suffering and pain will have proven that a world separated from God is a world that cannot fulfill our deepest needs and desires.

At some point in the near future—in the "days of these kings,"—Jesus will receive His kingdom and then come for His subjects.

"When the Son of Man comes in His glory, and all the holy angels with Him, then He will sit on the throne of His glory." (Matthew 25:31)

We are living on borrowed time.

---

2   Betty Radice, Ed. Herotodus: The Histories, p. 115.

3   You'll notice that in verse 41, Daniel makes a point of drawing our attention to the toes of the image.

4   The ten tribes, as they are commonly enumerated are as follows: Alemanni (Germans), Burgundians (Swiss), Franks (French), Anglo-Saxons (British), Suevi (Portuguese), Lombards (Italians), Visigoths (Spanish), Vandals, Ostrogoths, and the Heruli (these last three tribes are now extinct). Of course, the composition of Europe today is much broader than this, but the prophecy captures a moment in time shortly after the collapse of Rome.

5   www.sparknotes.com/biography/victoria/section10.rhtml

CHAPTER THREE

Planet in Upheaval

Standing on the Mount of Olives, the disciples had a perfect view of the temple. Admittedly, it was still a work in progress, but after forty-six years of hard labor, it was now a thing of beauty. Like a snowcap on a mountain, its brilliant white stones were a dazzling reflector of sunlight. It made everyone's heart swell with national pride. It was hard to believe that Jesus had predicted this temple would soon be desolate.

Concerned, one of the disciples approached Jesus. "Teacher," he said, "see what manner of stones and what buildings are here!" (Mark 13:1).

Like so many others, Jesus' followers had failed to grasp the real secret of the temple's glory. Although the architecture was magnificent, and the sacrificial rituals were dramatic, these were not the secret of its beauty.

Centuries earlier, the prophet Haggai had predicted, "the glory of this latter temple shall be greater than the former." It was a difficult prophecy to understand, given the fact that the Ark of the Covenant was still missing, and the Shekinah glory[6] had never graced this structure like it had in Solomon's day.[7] How would God fulfill this prediction?

Haggai's prophecy was pointing to the day when God would come to His temple in human flesh. In previous years, His glory had been hidden behind a veil in the innermost compartment of the temple, but now He stood among His people clothed in human flesh. God had become

Immanuel, "God with us." Never before had the glory of God's character been displayed so perfectly!

Sadly, as Jesus taught in the temple, much of His audience seemed to be ignorant or resentful of who He was. The common people were glad to listen to Him, and some of them were beginning to sense that He might be the long-awaited Messiah. To His disappointment, however, His teaching prompted harsh criticism from some of the highest religious authorities in the land. They would not accept Him. Finally, with tears in His eyes, He left. "Your house is left to you desolate," He said (Matthew 23:38). It would be both His last public message and His last visit to the temple.

Looking at the magnificent structure in the distance, the disciples were struggling to understand. Why would Jesus declare the temple desolate? Eagerly, the disciples waited for a response from their Master:

And Jesus said to them, "Do you not see all these things? Assuredly, I say to you, not one stone shall be left here upon another, that shall not be thrown down." (Matthew 24:2)

Jesus' prediction was fulfilled with remarkable accuracy. Work on the new temple was finally completed in 63 A.D., just seven years before Roman soldiers systematically destroyed it. During the siege of Titus on Jerusalem, his troops set the temple ablaze, and it was completely lost. When the fire finally died out, it occurred to the Romans that a considerable amount of the temple's gold had melted and run into cracks between the massive stones. Eager for plunder, they dismantled what was left of the building. Not one stone was left upon another—just as Jesus had predicted.

With the magnificent temple spread out below them, the disciples mulled over Jesus' words. It was hard to picture the temple in ruins, but they had to admit that it had happened before. If it were to crumble again, it would be an event of such significance that it would herald the end of the world. Maybe it would even signal the establishment of Jesus' new kingdom! They came back to Jesus with an important question:

Now as He sat upon the Mount of Olives, the disciples came to Him privately, saying, "Tell us, when will these things be? And what will be the sign of Your coming, and of the end of the age?" (Matthew 24:3)

In the original language of the gospels, the disciples use a word for Jesus' coming that is very important to the subject of this book: *parousia*.

The Bible uses it quite deliberately on several occasions. A *parousia* is an "appearance." It's a word that is often used of a king "arriving" or making a public appearance. More than a simple arrival, however, it implies a *presence*. A *parousia* is a little like a celebrity "making an entrance" at an important event. Your *parousia* is something everyone notices.

The disciples understood from the Scriptures that the Messiah was supposed to appear and establish a kingdom. In light of the frequency with which Jesus was speaking about His imminent departure, however, and His talk of the destruction of the temple, they were eager for some details. If Jesus was going to heaven, when would He reappear?

Jesus' answer was so profound that it has become a source of constant fascination for generations of Christian believers:

And Jesus answered and said to them: "Take heed that no one deceives you. For many will come in My name, saying, 'I am the Christ,' and will deceive many. And you will hear of wars and rumors of wars. See that you are not troubled; for all these things must come to pass, but the end is not yet. For nation will rise against nation, and kingdom against kingdom. And there will be famines, pestilences, and earthquakes in various places. All these are the beginning of sorrows." (Matthew 24: 4-8)

Jesus' answer is a list of events that will take place prior to His *parousia*. While these events do not provide a definite timeline, they do give us something to watch for.

When I was a little boy, my parents would sometimes take my brothers and me on long road trips. After we ran out of reading material and had been chastised for fighting a half dozen times, we would become exceptionally bored. About halfway through the trip we began to repeatedly ask one question: "Are we there yet?"

My parents, in their wisdom, gave us landmarks to watch for. "Before we get there, you're going to see a big lake on the left-hand side of the car." When we saw the lake, we would ask the question again. "Are we there yet?"

"Almost. Now watch for a big general store on the right-hand side of the road."

One by one, we would count the landmarks until we finally arrived at our destination. Each successive milestone would create a little more excitement. We didn't have an odometer in the back of the car, but we did have little events to watch for.

You'll notice that when the disciples asked about the timing of Jesus' kingdom, they weren't given an odometer. They weren't told that it would be a certain number of years until Christ returned. Instead, Jesus gave them something to watch for.

"Watch for these things—false Messiahs, wars, famines, pestilence and earthquakes," said Jesus. "When you see them, you'll know it's just about time for My *parousia*."

Critics of the Bible sometimes laugh at these words. They insist that these "signs" Jesus spoke of are of no value in predicting anything, because they are all things we live with every day. Sadly, even some Christian scholars have taken to criticizing Jesus' list. "Those things have always happened!" they point out. "We've always lived with war, pestilence, famine, earthquakes, and bad religion. These are not a reliable indicator of the times we live in!"

I'll give them partial credit for this comment. To some extent, they're right. We *have* always lived with those things. But the critics have not paid close attention to what Jesus actually said in verse 8: "All these are the beginning of *sorrows*." The word Matthew uses in the original language for *sorrows* is *odin*. Literally translated, it means "birth pains."

In other words, the signs of Christ's soon return will be like labor pains. The contractions will start out few and far between, but with the passage of time, they will increase in frequency and intensity. When they are quite severe, we can be sure that the time has come.

We will never be able to time the appearance of Jesus down to the day or year (Matthew 24:36; Acts 1:7), but the signs He gave us will provide a sure indication that we are drawing close:

"Now learn this parable from the fig tree: When its branch has already become tender and puts forth leaves, you know that summer is near. So you also, when you see all these things, know that it is near, at the very doors." (Matthew 24:32, 33)

In His wisdom, God has chosen not to reveal the exact timing of Christ's return to us. That's probably for the best, given our human nature. When I was a boy, my parents would occasionally go on a trip and leave me in charge of the house. Before they left, they always gave us a long list of chores designed to keep us out of trouble: we had to tend to the garden (we thought it was big enough to be named a "ranch"), chop endless piles of firewood, mow the lawn, do the dishes, and keep the house clean.

I was always flattered that my parents trusted me enough to give me such responsibility. My performance, however, seldom lived up to their expectations. Because we knew exactly which day to expect their return, most of the chores would be left completely undone until just a day or two before. Dirty dishes piled high in the sink. Soiled clothes littered the floor of the entire house. The grass grew until it qualified as hay. Within days of my parents' departure, the house became a certifiable disaster zone.

The day before my parents came back, we would suddenly spring into action and work like mad to disguise the fact that we had done absolutely nothing in their absence. Sometimes, we got away with it. Most of the time, we didn't.

God knows that sinful human beings are procrastinators by nature. If we knew the precise timing of the Second Coming, we might fall into the trap of believing that we can straighten out the mess in our lives a few days before Jesus comes, and all will be well. We could live like the devil and quickly "convert" a few days before He comes!

A good friend of mine tells the story of a little girl who had the messiest desk in her class. One afternoon, the teacher announced that she was going to give an award to the tidiest student.

"I'm going to win that award!" she proudly trumpeted.

The rest of the kids started laughing. "How could you possibly hope to win?" asked one little boy. "You're a pig! You've got the messiest desk in the school!"

She looked it over carefully and reluctantly determined that he was right. She thought the situation over, and then beamed from ear to ear as she thought of a solution.

"Well," she said, "the day before the inspection, I'll clean it up!"

"But what if the teacher checks the day before that?"

"Then I'll clean it up *two* days before the inspection," she said.

"And if the teacher checks the day before that?"

She furrowed her little brow for a moment. She breathed a discouraged sigh and said, "I guess I'll have to keep it clean all the time!"

It's probably best that we *don't* know when Jesus is coming. If we did, our religion might be built on all the wrong motives. We might live in fear of a deadline instead of resting in the loving relationship God wants us to have with Him. God wants us to focus more on Him than on deadlines. He wants us to be clean all the time—and He wants us to do it because *we* want to be clean.

I suspect that there are other reasons God does not provide a firm date. It's entirely possible that He hasn't picked one! Perhaps God is not measuring time in terms of years as much as He is measuring it in terms of *ripeness*.[8] Jesus often spoke of the Second Coming in terms of a harvest,[9] and you don't reap a harvest simply because it's time—you reap a harvest when it's ready.

Is it possible that God is waiting for certain conditions to be right? I believe so. Among other things, the Bible indicates that God is waiting until everyone who *might* choose Him makes a final decision for or against Him. (2 Peter 3:9) He also appears to be waiting for the character of Christ to be reproduced in His people. (See Matthew 25:31-40; John 17:20-23; Revelation 14:1-5)

The bottom line is this: we simply don't know when Jesus will arrive. We will know, however, when we're getting close.

Are there any indications that the labor pains Jesus spoke about are intensifying? Are we living in the time that Jesus spoke about? Skeptics love to point out that almost every generation has believed it would be the last, including civilizations that lived thousands of years ago. Some have quoted ancient passages like this one, found on an Assyrian tablet dating back to about 2800 B.C.:

> Our earth is degenerate in these latter days. There are signs that the world is speedily coming to an end. Bribery and corruption are common.[10]

Many people have suspected that their generation would be the last. For an ancient civilization to suspect that its moral fabric is unraveling, however, should come as no surprise. Every major civilization to have graced (or for that matter, *dis*graced) the face of the planet has eventually fallen into moral disrepair. Alexander the Great conquered the world, but died as a result of a degenerate personal life. The Roman Empire built great standards of justice and government, but collapsed in moral degeneracy. The great Babylonian civilization fell as Belshazzar, grandson to Nebuchadnezzar, hosted a reckless drunken feast. Many of the people who lived within those civilizations were able to recognize when the writing was on the wall.[11]

This is not the same thing, however, as noticing a worldwide increase in the signs Jesus told us to watch for. If we were only talking about one or two phenomena, we could dismiss them as the natural order of things—but the list that Jesus provides is so extensive that there will be no mistaking it. We will *know* when His coming is near.

Jesus told us to look for indications in three primary areas: the *religious* world, the *political* world, and the *natural* world.

Signs in the Religious World

In the field of religion, here's what Jesus told us to watch for:

"For many shall come in My name, saying, 'I am the Christ,' and will deceive many." (Matthew 24:5)

"Then if anyone says to you, 'Look, here is the Christ!' or 'There!' do not believe it. For false christs and false prophets will arise and show great signs and wonders, so as to deceive, if possible, even the elect. See, I have told you beforehand. Therefore if they say to you, 'Look, He is in the desert!' do not go out; or 'Look, He is in the inner rooms!' do not believe it. For as the lightning comes from the east and flashes to the west, so also will the coming of the Son of Man be." (Matthew 24: 23-28)

Throughout history, there have always been one or two fanatics here or there who developed a Messiah complex and managed to convince others that they were Jesus. These people have always been few and far between—until recent years. It now happens so often that there's a clinical name for it: *Jerusalem Syndrome.*

What is Jerusalem Syndrome? As the change of the millennium approached a few years ago, people started flocking to Jerusalem in droves, certain that the year 2000 was a religious landmark. A rather large number of tourists were discovered walking the streets of the city dressed in outfits reminiscent of John the Baptist or Jesus. Apparently, such a large number of these people were convinced that they were the Messiah or some other biblical character that the name *Jerusalem Syndrome* was coined to describe the growing problem.[12]

It's one thing to convince yourself that you are Christ; it's quite another to convince somebody else of it. In recent decades, however, a disturbing number of people have managed to pull it off. Jim Jones of the People's temple managed to do it. Thousands lost their lives after drinking Kool-Aid laced with cyanide. Unbelievably, Charles Manson still has a following of people who are convinced that he is Christ. Some of them are serving time for murders he asked them to commit. The Reverend Sun Myung Moon (Unification Church), whose followers number in thousands, has declared that Jesus failed in His mission, and that he (Moon) is divine. David Koresh persuaded his followers that he was a "sinful Christ" before they perished in flames at the Mount Carmel complex. David Applewhite (Heaven's Gate Cult) managed to convince his followers that he was a new incarnation of Jesus.

The list goes on. Unbelievably, some people who monitor cults estimate that the number of people in North America who believe themselves to be Christ *and have a following* is now well over 1,200. Compared to the one or two scattered through history, that number is staggering. Are the contractions getting stronger? Absolutely.

In addition to the extreme cases of religious delusion, the Bible also provides a subtler hint that time is running out. Religion itself will turn sour:

But know this, that in the last days perilous times will come: for men will be lovers of themselves, lovers of money, boasters, proud, blasphemers, disobedient to parents, unthankful, unholy, unloving, unforgiving, slanderers, without self-control, brutal, despisers of good, traitors, headstrong, haughty, lovers of pleasure more than lovers of God, having a form of godliness, but denying its power…. (2 Timothy 3: 1-5a)

The generation that lives just prior to Christ's return will be completely self-absorbed. Money and possessions will be the highest priority. Respect for authority will vanish. Promises and covenants will be worthless, including the marriage covenant. Essentially, many people—even those who profess Christianity—will lack self-control.

At the same time, Paul points out, these people will continue to profess religion, but they will merely be going through the motions. They have a "form of godliness," but deny its power. They claim to know God, but they don't really believe His Word.

Nowhere has this become more evident than in 21st century North American Christianity. Just a generation ago, most children of Christian parents were raised to know and believe the Bible, but that no longer appears to be true. A relatively recent Gallup poll I stumbled across posed four questions to church-going Christians. The results were staggering:

1. *Is there such a thing as absolute moral truth?*
    47% said *no.*

2. *Is there such a thing as the Holy Spirit?*
    43% said *no.*

3. *Did Jesus literally rise from the dead?*
   33% said *no.*

4. *Did Jesus ever sin while He was here on earth?*
   19% said *yes.*

These are not minor issues. These represent core beliefs of the Christian faith. Those who were interviewed were not atheists or secular humanists—they were faithful churchgoers! Skepticism born in the minds of critics at ivory-tower institutions has made its way into the pews of North American churches.

Everywhere I travel, people are sensing a tremendous emptiness in their spiritual lives, even though they are active members of churches. Something has turned sour in the world of religion—millions of people are going through the motions of a spiritual life, but lack any real spiritual power in their day-to-day lives.

In some corners of Christianity, church has become a matter of entertainment to make up for the spiritual lack people are noticing in their lives. In a last-ditch effort to keep people in the pews, the worship service is altered to the point where it resembles a sales convention more than a church service. Christianity becomes more about worldly prosperity than selfless service, more about self-improvement than about Jesus Christ. The focus has drifted away from the sinner's need of the cross of Christ and the kingdom of heaven, to self. Repentance from sin has become a taboo subject; if church doesn't "do something for us," we quickly lose interest.

That's not to say that God isn't concerned about our well-being. Does the Christian faith broaden your horizons and improve your quality of life? Undoubtedly. Yet those things are the side dish, not the main course. The Christian faith is first and foremost about Jesus Christ and a powerful, saving relationship with Him.

At one point in His ministry, Jesus asked a painful question: "When the Son of Man comes, will He find faith on the earth?" (Luke 18:8). Fortunately, the answer to the question is *yes*. In vision, John is shown a special last-day group of people who have persisted with a stubborn faith that did not wilt in the face of skepticism or last-day religious deceptions:

These are the ones who follow the Lamb wherever he goes. These were redeemed from among men, being firstfruits to God and to the Lamb. And in their mouth was found no guile, for they are without fault before the throne of God. (Revelation 14:4b, 5)

There will be people who are following Christ when He appears. The question for each of us, then, is this: as we search the scriptures and search our hearts, will we discover that we are a part of this group? It's an important question, because the Bible indicates—quite strongly, I might add—that there will be a massive religious deception blanketing the earth just prior to Christ's appearance. In the thirteenth chapter of the book of Revelation, John tells us about a miracle-working power that will lead most of the world into a dangerously false religious experience.

Are there any labor pains in the religious world? Absolutely—and they're getting stronger with each passing day.

Signs in the Political World

In addition to religious signs, Jesus also warned that there would be considerable tremors in the political world:

And you will hear of wars and rumors of wars. See that you are not troubled; for all these things must come to pass, but the end is not yet. For nation will rise against nation, and kingdom against kingdom. (Matthew 24:6,7a)

The human race has suffered the ravages of war as long as anyone can remember. In the entire recorded history of the world, there have only been a handful of years when a war has not been fought somewhere on the planet. In recent years, however, the intensity and frequency of warfare has been rising dramatically.

That comes as a surprise to a lot of people, particularly those who live in the Western World. We tend to think that we live in a time of relative peace, but nothing could be further from the truth. One of our biggest problems is that we've gotten very good at war. A battle that used to be fought with clubs, spears and arrows is now fought with laser-guided missiles and multi-million dollar fighter jets. We can kill tens of thousands of people in a heartbeat without ever having to look our opponent in the eye.

History will record the twentieth century as one of the bloodiest periods in the story of humanity. More than 200 million people died as a result of military combat. Two global wars, fought on a scale never before seen by mankind, were responsible for a significant portion of that number. During the First World War, 10 million people sacrificed their lives on the battlefields of Europe.

The devastation was so terrible that those who fought it dubbed it "the war to end all wars," because it was impossible to imagine that humanity is capable of anything worse. The Second World War proved them wrong; it ended with a single bomb that wiped out an entire metropolis. We have become the first generation that is actually capable of destroying the entire planet in a heartbeat.

The carnage has not all been due to malevolent technology, however. Some of the twentieth century's bloodiest battles were fought with less than high-tech weapons. Recently, I visited the nation of Rwanda, where nearly one million people were put to death with machetes and clubs in the space of three months in 1995. By comparison, the Nazi death camps eliminated approximately six million Jews during the entire Second World War.

Our team visited a little village about an hour outside of the capital city of Kigali, where more than 20,000 people lost their lives in a single day of genocide. At the edge of the community is a now-abandoned church, where it is estimated that 10,000 people were butchered in one day.

The sanctuary is no longer used for church services, because it has been converted into a genocide memorial. For ten years, the government allowed the bodies to remain where they fell as a painful reminder of the depth of depravity of which human nature is capable.

As we stepped inside the church, the wind was whistling mournfully through bullet holes in the roof. A pile of rotting clothes, soaked with blood, was stacked up in one corner. The walls, floor and church furniture were stained dark with massive bloodstains. The bones of the victims, too many to number, are now buried in a crypt behind the church.

Perhaps the most tragic story of all is the fact that God's house was used as an instrument of destruction. Thousands of people, desperate for refuge, fled to churches seeking asylum. Their place of sanctuary became a death trap when even the sanctity of a place of worship was ignored by bloodthirsty mobs.

We might choose to believe that we live in an era of relative peace, but we would be living in denial. From the Korea and Vietnam wars to the war in Iraq, the world has not had much of a breather in the past few decades. Corrupted minds toy with newer and nastier ways of killing people. Terrorist bombings are a regular feature in the evening news. Millions around the planet live with the threat of violence every day.

Every year, the nations of the civilized world spend untold billions of dollars on war preparations, even now that the Cold War is officially over. In some ways, the collapse of the Soviet Union has made the world a much less secure place to live. Small, renegade nations with a political or religious axe to grind are acquiring nuclear technology. Yet, in some ways, the most expensive weapons are not the most frightening ones. In recent years, there has been an alarming shift away from the nuclear arms race to a less expensive and far more sinister option: biological warfare.

The specter of biological weapons, first developed in the middle of last century, had lain dormant until immediately after the collapse of the World Trade Center. Shortly after that devastating terrorist attack, someone started sending Anthrax powder to prominent Americans through the U.S. postal system. It was an inexpensive way to paralyze an entire nation with fear. Opening your mail was suddenly a potentially lethal activity.

The anthrax mailings eventually tapered off, but the threat has by no means disappeared. Shortly after the attacks, a story aired on PBS's *Nova* that revealed how simple it is to acquire biological weapons. A manufacturing center can be set up with readily available equipment for a few thousand dollars, and a widespread assault can be launched with something as simple as a crop-duster.

There may not be a need, however, for a terrorist to manufacture his own biological agents. Apparently, there are plenty of them available on the black market. The city of Stepnogorsk, located in Kazakhstan, was a secret community built from the ground up in 1982 by the government of the former Soviet Union. In clear violation of treaty agreements, it was specifically designed for the production of biological weapons.

One former employee stated that the scientists at Stepnogorsk produced enough biological agents to kill off the entire human population nine or ten times over. When the Soviet Union collapsed, the city was abandoned, but much of the biological material produced there remained behind. The abandoned plant lies just a few miles north of the Afghanistan border—in easy reach of terrorist groups.

While efforts have been made to change the situation at Stepnogorsk, the recent use of anthrax on an unsuspecting public raises a very real concern. Where have all the custom disease agents that were manufactured there over the last fifty years gone? Do we know where they are? Is it possible that terrorist cells have access to them?

Personally, I do not live in fear of such threats. The worst that man has to offer cannot possibly compare with the best that Christ has planned for us when He returns. One day, war will only be a distant memory as we walk the streets of paradise. God was the first One to experience the devastating effects of war (see Revelation 12:7), and He has both a desire and a plan to put an end to it. Until that time comes, however, Jesus warns us that there will be a dramatic increase in warfare. The human race will push the envelope of its destructive potential to the limit.

Signs in the Natural World

Along with the increase in warfare and bad religion, there will be a number of natural phenomena to watch for:

And there will be famines, pestilences, and earthquakes in various places. (Matthew 24:7b)

It's hard for people living in the over-fed west to imagine that most of the world does not get enough to eat. While we count calories and struggle to keep our weight down, approximately four out of five of the world's children are born into families that simply cannot afford to feed them. Every six seconds a child dies of starvation and, around the world, 230 million children suffer stunted growth because of malnutrition. More than one billion people—nearly one in six—cannot meet their basic nutritional needs.

Famine has always been a part of the human experience, but not on the scale the world is witnessing today. Perhaps one of the most tragic aspects of world hunger is the fact that we have enough resources, globally speaking, to feed everyone, yet most of the world still goes to bed hungry each night. With uncontrollable population growth in some developing nations, the problem promises to get much, much worse in coming years.

When you add pestilence to hunger, the suffering becomes much worse. Many of the diseases we thought had been eliminated are now making a comeback. For example, the Black Death (or "the plague") recently reared its ugly head in the streets of Gujurat state in India. New strains of treatment-resistant tuberculosis are making their rounds in North America. Add to this list the Ebola virus (which has accidentally touched down in North America at least once), mad cow disease, West Nile Virus, Streptococcus A (the flesh-eating disease), and the collection of modern super-diseases becomes quite frightening.

Jean and I were living in Toronto when the deadly SARS virus broke out. The news quickly circulated that if you had flu-like symptoms, you were to be isolated for a period of ten days to be sure you were not infected. Visits to the hospital, where the bulk of new infections seemed to be taking place, were strictly regulated. If by chance you were permitted to go inside, you were carefully surveyed and then masked and gowned. The airport was outfitted with special infrared equipment designed to identify people in security line-ups who had a fever.

Understandably, everyone was nervous. No one was sure how to handle the sudden epidemic, because *nobody had ever seen the disease before*. It was brand-new—introduced into the human population from the meat-markets of Asia.

During the 1980s, the airwaves were buzzing with news of another relatively new disease: AIDS. Today, the AIDS epidemic might not make the evening news like it used to, but it is still growing at an alarming rate. Worldwide, at the moment of this writing, an estimated 40 million people are living with AIDS.[13] In 2004, three million people lost their lives to the disease, and five million new cases were reported. Some of the worst areas of infection are found in sub-Saharan Africa, where an estimated 25 million people have been infected with the killer virus. At current rates of infection, AIDS could infect 89 million Africans by the year 2025.[14] The HIV prevalence rate has reached more than 35% in nations like Botswana and Swaziland.

To make matters worse, the disease appears to be mutating. In February of 2005, a new variant of AIDS was discovered in a patient that resists 19 out of the 20 anti-retroviral drugs traditionally used to treat the disease. It moves much more quickly than the original disease, which may linger in a person's body for a decade before making itself known.

We have always lived with frightening diseases. The plague wiped out a huge portion of Europe's population in the Dark Ages. Outbreaks of cholera have devastated countless populations in the past. But never before have so many new diseases appeared all at once, with so few possibilities for treatment. Are the contractions coming more closely together?

Earthquakes

I grew up in a place that was seismically active, yet we seldom felt any real earthquakes growing up. At most, we noticed occasionally that the hanging plants in the house were gently swaying. When I moved to Toronto, however, an amazing thing happened one afternoon as I was sitting at my desk. There was a loud rumbling noise, and my desk suddenly jumped. At first I thought a large truck must have accidentally backed into the building, but I was wrong. It was an earthquake—in a place I didn't really expect to experience one!

Across the planet, there are thousands of little tremors that take place every day as fault lines shift. Most of them are too small to detect, so they go unnoticed by all but those who happen to have a seismograph at their disposal.

In the last moments before His appearing, however, Jesus assures us that we will notice many of them. The final natural sign of His coming is an increase in earthquakes in "various places".

A few years ago, I decided to see if earthquakes were really on the rise. I went to the geology section of a large university library and started to sort through the books. What I discovered was very interesting: no two geologists seemed to agree on just how many large earthquakes this world has experienced over the last few centuries.

Part of the problem is that different authors use different criteria to define what constitutes a "large" earthquake. I *did* notice an interesting pattern, however. No matter which criteria you apply, the number of earthquakes since the days of Christ appears to be on the rise.

Let me give you an example. When I paged through one major seismography textbook, I decided to jot down all of the earthquakes that had caused significant damage, such as destruction of property and loss of human lives.[15] Through the centuries since the New Testament was written, there appear to have been one or two such quakes per century. In the seventeenth century, the number suddenly jumped to six. In the eighteenth century, it was thirteen. The nineteenth century produced twenty-six such quakes, and the twentieth century had more than one hundred!

At the moment this book is being written, the world is still reeling from the deaths of nearly 300,000 people who lost their lives when a massive undersea earthquake triggered a tsunami that washed over a significant portion of Asia. This earthquake caused such devastation that it demanded our attention—yet so many destructive quakes take place each year now that they scarcely make headlines.

The world is not the same place it used to be. It's getting difficult to define what "normal" weather is. As I write these words, scores of houses in "sunny" Southern California are sliding off hillsides because of record-breaking torrential rains. Four hurricanes in rapid succession recently slammed into the Caribbean and the east coast of America. Places that used to be cold in winter are warming up, and places that used to be warm are becoming cold.

Is it possible that the labor pains Jesus spoke of nearly 2,000 years ago are beginning to peak? Things could conceivably get much worse, and time could drag on for years—but the leaves on the fig tree appear to be sprouting. Labor pains are increasing with each passing day. The time for Christ's appearing is quickly approaching.

---

6   Shekinah is a word often used to describe the literal presence of God over the Ark of the Covenant.

7   See 2 Chronicles 7:1-3

8   That having been said, there is no question that there are definite time elements in the Bible, such as Daniel's seventy weeks. We'll take a look at that prophecy in a coming chapter.

9 See, for example, Matthew 13:37-43 and Revelation 14:14-16

10 Isaac Asimov, Book of Facts, p. 35

11 This expression, of course, literally comes from the event that announced the imminent fall of Babylon the night that Cyrus took the city. See Daniel chapter five.

12 Interestingly, Christians tend to believe that they are John the Baptist or some other biblical figure, and Jews who fall prey to this temporary insanity seem to believe that they are a Messianic figure.

13 See the UN's website at http://www.unaids.org/EN/resources/epidemiology.asp

14 Lawrence K. Altman, A UN Report Takes a Hard Look at Fighting AIDS in Africa, New York Times: March 5, 2005

15 I did this deliberately, since it is often argued that before the invention of the seismograph, people couldn't keep good records of earthquakes. They always managed to notice, however, when their house was collapsing!

CHAPTER FOUR

The Appearing

"What do you *mean*, it's not in there?" I couldn't believe it. Moving to The United States was proving to be much more of an administrative nightmare than I had expected. Just the night before, I had called the Social Security administration to ask whether or not my new Social Security number had arrived. They assured me that it had, but that for security reasons, they couldn't give it to me over the telephone. I would have to come in person to collect it.

"Has my wife's number also arrived?" They checked the computer and assured me that Jean's new number was also there.

We were among the first people to line up outside the office the next morning. When we stepped up to the counter, my number was ready as promised, but as much as they fiddled with their computer, they couldn't find Jean's.

"Are you sure you've applied for a number?" one clerk asked.

"Of course!" we said, "And last night someone here told us they found it."

"Well, it's not here now!"

Mildly frustrated, we took a seat and waited for the clerks to figure out what had happened. As time began to drag by, my two small children began exploring the waiting room. Eventually, they made friends with the security guard—a middle-aged man sitting comfortably in a chair near the door.

After a few moments, I went to pry my kids off him. With a smile, he asked me what I did for a living.

"I'm a minister," I told him. Almost immediately, he perked up.

"You're a minister?" he asked. "Then maybe you can help me with something. My son and I have been discussing the Second Coming of Christ, and I'm a little confused about it. Some people say it's going to happen one way, and other people say something else. Do you think you could show me from the Bible what it actually says?"

He pulled a little Bible out of his coat pocket. By looking at it, I could tell that he had read it many times.

"I know your frustration," I said. "It seems as if no two Christians can agree on this subject—but if you've got a little time, I can show you some things we know beyond the shadow of a doubt."

Together, for the next half hour or so, we turned to various passages, allowing scripture to speak for itself. He was pleasantly surprised at how clearly the subject presents itself if you take the time to gather all of the relevant passages in the Bible and read them together.

In this chapter, let's take a look at some of the basic passages from the Bible that describe the return of Jesus Christ. As we move through them, some people will undoubtedly drop each passage into one of two file folders in their minds: (1) Christ's return for His church, and (2) Christ's glorious return to establish His kingdom. I have chosen to look at those distinctions later, and I'm sure you'll see why when we get there. For now, however, let's simply allow the Bible to speak for itself:

(1) One of the first things we know about the return of Christ is that it will be an **audible** event. When Jesus comes, you're going to *hear* it. The apostle Paul makes this quite clear in his first letter to the Thessalonian church:

*For the Lord Himself will descend from heaven **with a shout**, with **the voice of an archangel**, and with **the trumpet of God**. And the dead in Christ shall rise first. (1 Thessalonians 4:16)*

There are three audible events in this verse: (1) a shout, (2) the voice of the archangel, and (3) the trumpet of God. Apparently, these events are loud enough to wake the dead! Other prophetic passages reinforce this idea. Consider the words of the Psalmist:

*Our God shall come, **and shall not keep silent**; A fire shall devour before Him, and it shall be very tempestuous all around Him. (Ps. 50:3)*

And consider these words from Jesus Himself:

*And He will send His angels with **a great sound of a trumpet**, and they will gather together His elect from the four winds, from one end of heaven to the other. (Matthew 24:31)*

The noise generated by the Second Coming will not be insignificant. Jesus will not come with a whisper—He will come with a "great sound."

(2) The next thing we know for sure is that Christ's return will be a **visible** event. When Jesus comes, you're going to *see* it:

*Then the sign of the Son of Man will appear in heaven, and then all the tribes of the earth will mourn, and **they will see the Son of Man** coming on the clouds of heaven with power and great glory. (Matthew 24:30)*

*For as the **lightning comes from the east and flashes to the west**, so also will the coming of the Son of Man be. (Matthew 24:27)*

*Behold, He is coming with clouds, **and every eye will see Him**, and they also who pierced Him. And all the tribes of the earth will mourn because of Him. Even so, Amen. (Revelation 1:7)*

When Jesus returns, you won't have to check the evening news to catch up on what happened. You won't have to refer to courtroom sketches for details. You're going to see it for yourself.

This detail is much more important than you might think. There is a modern tendency to explain away what the Bible says about the Second Coming of Jesus as a personal, private event. Some people teach that the Second Coming takes place on a personal level when you have a religious experience. At that moment, the theory says, Jesus comes to you personally.

I have no question that people experience personal encounters with Christ, or that He makes Himself known to people. I know for a fact that it happens. That is *not* the Second Coming of Christ spoken of in the Bible, however. When Jesus returns, *everyone is going to see it*.

That simple fact also rules out the considerable number of Messianic imposters in our world who claim to be the Christ:

"Then if anyone says to you, 'Look, here is the Christ!' or 'There!' do not believe it. For false christs and false prophets will arise and show great signs and wonders, so as to deceive, if possible, even the elect. See, I have told you beforehand. Therefore if they say to you, 'Look, He is in

the desert!' do not go out; or 'Look, He is in the inner rooms!' do not believe it." (Matthew 24:23-26)

Countless lives could have been saved if people had only taken this passage to heart before signing up with some apocalyptic cult. David Koresh claimed to be Christ, but his claim contradicts the words of Jesus Himself that every eye will see Him when He returns. Marshall Applewhite of the Heaven's Gate cult also claimed to be Christ, but I don't remember witnessing his arrival. Jim Jones laid claim to Messianic status, but the whole world didn't see him appear. Those who chose to follow these men paid for it with their lives. They would still be alive if they had read the words of Christ Himself: there will be no private appearances for select groups of people. When Jesus comes, everybody will see it.

(3) When Jesus returns, it will be the **end of world history** as we know it. When Jesus appears, every bar will have served its last drink. Every hospital will have treated its last patient. Every unsolved file at the police station will be closed forever.

When you hear the trumpet blast and look up to see the Son of God returning in the clouds, the final chapter of your life will have been written. It will be too late to change the record or add an amendment, because Christ has returned to hand out final rewards:

"For the Son of Man will come in the glory of His Father with His angels, and then He will reward each according to his works." (Matthew 16:27)

Finally, there is laid up for me the crown of righteousness, which the Lord, the righteous Judge, will give to me on that Day, and not to me only but also to all who have loved His appearing. (2 Timothy 4:8)

"And behold, I am coming quickly, and My reward is with Me, to give every one according to his work." (Revelation 22:12)

For some people, the sound of trumpets will strike terror in their hearts. When they look up and see Jesus coming, they will know that time has run out. It's too late to make things right with God. The sixth chapter of Revelation records their tragic reaction to Christ's appearance:

And the kings of the earth, the great men, the rich men, the chief commanders, the mighty men, every slave, and every free man, hid themselves in the caves and in the rocks of the mountains, and said to the mountains and rocks, "Fall on us and hide us from the face of Him who sits on the throne and from the wrath of the Lamb! For the great day of His wrath has come, and who is able to stand?" (Revelation 6:15, 16)

There is nothing worse than taking an important test you haven't prepared for. I remember one such occasion from my university experience. As the final exam was distributed, I was well aware that I had not read my assignments or studied the class notes. I whispered a silent prayer that the questions would be easy, but my worst fears were realized when I turned the paper over and read the first question. I barely understood what it was talking about!

Beads of sweat broke out on my forehead, and I skipped to the next question in hope of finding something I could answer. It was just as bad. I desperately racked my brain looking for something intelligent I could say about each subject, but nothing was forthcoming. Three hours slipped by quickly, and the bell suddenly rang as I was half way through the second question. Time was up!

The proctor came around to collect our work. There was no use pleading for more time; most of the students were quite well prepared because they had taken advantage of the entire semester to prepare for this moment. Many of them left with telling smiles on their faces. I left with my head hanging. I knew I had failed.

The real tragedy of those who are caught unprepared when Jesus comes is the amount of time they have had to respond to God's call. Heaven has turned over every stone in an effort to get them to respond to God's invitation. When they hear the trumpet blast, a shiver of terror will run through their bodies, because they know they haven't prepared.

As they glance around, however, they notice that not everyone is terrified. Many people have broad smiles on their faces—they're actually glad for this event!

And it will be said in that day: "Behold, this is our God; we have waited for Him, and he will save us. This is the LORD; we have waited for Him; we will be glad and rejoice in His salvation." (Isaiah 25:9)

There will be two groups of people when Christ returns—those who shout for joy, and those who scream in terror. Both of them know that time is up—it's too late to change your mind. The difference between them is what they have chosen to do with Christ's free gift of salvation during their lives.

(4) When Jesus returns, it will be the **same Jesus** that the disciples knew and loved. This is a point that cannot be overemphasized. Some religious groups have tried to convince the world that Jesus has already come in a mystical or spiritual sense. This is *not* what the authors of the Bible had in mind when they spoke of the Second Coming. They believed that the real, physical Jesus who taught them and walked among them would come back in person.

This becomes quite evident when you consider the story of Christ's resurrection. After the crucifixion, the disciple Thomas had a little trouble believing that Jesus had actually returned from the dead:

But Thomas, called Didymus, one of the twelve, was not with them when Jesus came. The other disciples therefore said to him, "We have seen the Lord." But he said to them, "Unless I see in His hands the print of the nails, and put my finger into the print of the nails, and put my hand into His side, I will not believe."

And after eight days His disciples were again inside, and Thomas with them. Jesus came, the doors being shut, and stood in the midst, and said, "Peace to you!" Then He said to Thomas, "Reach your finger here, and look at My hands; and reach your hand here, and put it into My side. Do not be unbelieving, but believing." And Thomas answered and said to Him, "My Lord and my God!" Jesus said to him, "Thomas, because you have seen Me, you have believed. Blessed are those who have not seen and yet have believed." (John 20:24-29)

This is an important story that sheds a lot of light on the Second Coming. When Jesus appeared to the disciples after the resurrection, He made a point of demonstrating that He had physically risen from the dead. He had a real body of flesh and bones. (Luke 24:39) Even before His encounter with Thomas, Jesus showed His hands and side to the rest of the disciples. (John 20:20) He also made a point of eating something in front of them. (Luke 24:42, 43) According to the Bible, He provided a *lot* of proof. (Acts 1:3) The point Jesus was making was abundantly clear: He had literally risen from the dead.

What does that have to do with the Second Coming? Everything. Jesus rose from the dead in a real human body. He has chosen— remarkably—to remain a part of the human family for all time. He now stands in heaven's sanctuary as a representative of the human race. (Hebrews 4:14-16) While He is fully God, He is also fully human.

When Jesus ascended into heaven, He went with a physical body. The Bible teaches that when He returns, He will come back the same way:

*Now when He had spoken these things, while they watched, He was taken up, and a cloud received Him out of their sight. And while they looked steadfastly toward heaven as He went up, behold, two men stood by them in white apparel, who also said, "Men of Galilee, why do you stand gazing up into heaven? **This same Jesus**, who was taken up from you into heaven, **will so come in like manner** as you saw Him go into heaven." (Acts 1:9-11)*

Pay close attention to what the angels told the disciples. The Jesus that went to heaven is the *same* Jesus who will return—and He will come in the same manner they saw Him go. These two simple facts teach us a lot about the return of Christ. He literally ascended into heaven; He will literally come back. He went to heaven with a physical human body; He will return with the same one.

I have heard religious groups claim that Christ has already returned spiritually and invisibly. Other groups have argued that the return of Christ has already occurred through the activities of the church. All of these groups are in error, because the Bible teaches a literal, physical coming of Christ.

When Jesus appears, there will be no mistaking it. A loud shout and trumpet blast will demand our attention. Christ will return in the glory of His Father with all the holy angels, and the graves of believers will open as ancient Christians come back to life. Nobody will miss this event!

In this chapter, we have explored a number of important texts that describe the return of Jesus Christ. *Before you move on to the next chapter*, take some time to review them all carefully. This is important. Let the Bible authors plainly speak for themselves. Avoid the temptation to read things into the passages that simply aren't there. Pay attention to little details. Read the verses aloud. Mentally place yourself in the context in which they were written. Ask yourself if there's anything you haven't noticed before.

Then get ready to dive into a serious exploration of Bible prophecy.

CHAPTER FIVE

A Thief in the Night

Walk into any Christian bookstore, and you'll make a remarkable discovery. There are as many different opinions written on Bible prophecy, as there are books. One theory, however, dominates the modern marketplace of ideas. It runs a little like this (with admitted variations):

Abruptly, without warning, millions of believers suddenly disappear. Drivers seem to evaporate from behind the wheels of their cars. Airplanes start dropping out of the sky because the pilots have vanished. The world is stunned; few people realize what has just happened. Jesus has at long last come for His church and secretly removed it from the planet so that His people do not need to pass through the coming tribulation.

Christians are relocated to heaven to be with Christ; the nation of Israel becomes the primary focus of God's attention for the next seven years. Foreign invaders are miraculously turned or stopped as they attack Israel. The final week of Daniel's 70-week prophecy has begun!

Now that the restraining power of the Holy Spirit has been removed from the earth (because the church is gone), the devil is able to swing into full gear. The Antichrist rises to power, and makes a peace-treaty with the nation of Israel. After three and a half years the treaty is broken, and the Antichrist declares himself to be God and demands the worship of the whole planet. Millions are forced to take the Mark of the Beast.

All is not lost, however, because some people refuse to take the Mark.

There is a growing movement among the Jews to turn to Christ. Many of them convert, and become last-minute evangelists who prepare the world for Jesus to come in glory and establish His kingdom on earth. Faced with relentless persecution by the forces of the Antichrist, they must work in the world's most trying circumstances. Finally, the power of the Antichrist is ultimately broken when Christ returns in glory and destroys him.

This general timeline of last-day events has been tremendously popular for a few generations, the most recent presentation of it being the wildly popular *Left Behind* series. Admittedly, a lot of people who read the previous four paragraphs are going to find it a little simplistic, and some will disagree with a few of the details. Overall, however, it paints a fairly accurate picture of the most popular timetable of last-day events. If it were portrayed in chart format, it would look something like this:

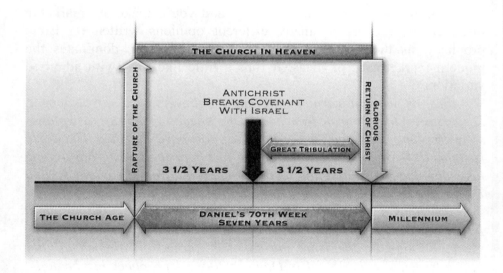

One of the most exciting events in the sequence, of course, is the moment that Jesus comes for His church. Many Christians refer to this event as the *rapture*, which is a word that is not found in the Bible. Some have referred to it as the "secret" rapture because nobody but the Christians saw what happened. The word "rapture" is derived from a Latin translation of the Greek word *harpadzo*, and simply means "to be caught up," or "to snatch away."

The concept comes from Paul's first letter to the church in Thessalonica, where he describes the coming of Christ as a moment when the church is "caught up" to be with Christ:

Then we who are alive and remain shall be caught up together with them in the clouds to meet the Lord in the air. And thus we shall always be with the Lord. (1 Thessalonians 4:17)

Christians who subscribe to the "secret rapture" theory of Christ's coming usually present His return in two separate phases. First, Jesus comes to "snatch away" His church so that they do not have to endure the Antichrist or the tribulation period, and then seven years later, Christ comes again in glory to establish His kingdom. Popular prophecy authors Tim LaHaye and Jerry B. Jenkins describe it this way:

First, He will come suddenly in the air to rapture His church and take believers to His Father's house, in fulfillment of His promise in John 14:1-3. There they will appear before the judgment seat of Christ (2 Corinthians 5:8-10) and participate in the marriage supper of the Lamb (Revelation 19:1-10). Second, He will finish his second coming by returning to earth gloriously and publicly in great power to set up His kingdom.[16]

This theory is sometimes referred to as the "two phase" coming of Christ. When the first phase of Christ's return takes place, most of the world doesn't know what happened. The only thing they know is that millions of people have mysteriously disappeared, and world leaders concoct a story to explain the widespread disappearances. Only a tiny band of people suspects the truth, because even though they were unprepared for Christ to come, they knew what the Bible said.

Understanding the Theory

There are a number of important concepts taught by those who subscribe to this popular theory:

(1) The coming of Christ is *imminent*. Jesus could come at any moment, for any generation, because there are no prophecies that must be fulfilled before He comes. The church is waiting for nothing at this point except the rapture.

This stems from the belief that the last seven years of earth's history are really the last week of Daniel's 70-week prophecy (we'll take a look at this a little later). God's prophetic clock stopped at the beginning of the Christian era, at the end of the first 69 weeks of Daniel's prophecy. It will start again once the church disappears.

The entire church age is a 2,000-year insertion into God's prophetic timetable that the Old Testament prophets couldn't see. If the prophets couldn't see the Christian church, they also didn't provide us with any prophetic events to watch for. Thus Christ could come at any moment, without warning.

The rapture of the church must therefore take place before the appearance of the Antichrist or the tribulation period, because the prophets clearly saw those events.

(2) Most of the book of Revelation does not apply to the Christian church today. It has been pointed out that the words "church" and "churches" are used thirty times in the first three chapters of Revelation. In chapter four, however, John's attention is suddenly directed toward heaven, and the church is not mentioned again. This is because the Christian church has been taken to heaven and no longer resides on the earth.

Chapters four and five are a description of the church in heaven, and then chapters six through nineteen are a description of events that take place on earth after the rapture, during the last seven years of earth's history.

In his best-selling book of yesteryear, *The Late Great Planet Earth,* Hal Lindsey elaborates:

> The largest descriptive volume of the Tribulation is found in Revelation 6 through 19. Here is a fascinating revelation about Revelation. In the first five chapters of this book, the church is mentioned thirty times. In fact, in chapters 2 and 3, and the end of each letter to the churches, John says "let him hear what the Spirit saith unto the churches." This is repeated seven times. Then we have the beginning of the description of the Tribulation, and there is not one mention of the churches. Why? Because the church will be in heaven at that time.[17]

(3) The Holy Spirit, through the Christian church, is the restraining power mentioned in 2 Thessalonians 2:7. Once the church has been evacuated from the earth, there is nothing left to hold back the forces of evil. The absence of the church thus paves the way for the appearance of the Antichrist, who deals treacherously with the nation of Israel. (It is thus understood that the Antichrist will only make his appearance after the rapture.)

(4) God will not require the church to go through the tribulation. Christian believers will be spared from earth's worst moments, because they are safely removed to heaven.

(5) Every time the Bible speaks of Israel, it means the literal nation of Israel, even in the New Testament. (Note extensive coverage of this theory in chapter ten.)

(6) Christ's millennial (thousand-year) reign will be on earth, after the great tribulation. In some versions of the theory, this will be a time when Christ rules the world with a rod of iron. Christians will reign with Christ over those who are not Christians. Sin and death still exist. Take, for example, the scenario laid out by Tim LaHaye in his *Popular Encyclopedia of Bible Prophecy:*

> The millennium will be a time of both political and spiritual rule. Politically, it will be universal (Daniel 2:35), authoritative (Isaiah 11:4), and characterized by righteousness and justice, with assurances for the poor (Isaiah 11:3-5), and admonition and judgment for the violators of Messiah's rule (Psalm 2:10-12).
>
> This literal earthly reign of Christ will also have spiritual characteristics. First and foremost it will be a reign of righteousness in which Christ will be King, reigning in absolute righteousness (Isaiah 32:1). It will also be a time when the fullness of the Spirit and the holiness of God will be manifested (Isaiah 11:2-5)....
>
> Everything from work to worship will be holy. Sin will be punished (Psalm 72:1-4; Zechariah 14:16-21) in an open, just way.[18]

Although only the redeemed will go into the Messiah's kingdom, the living saints from the Tribulation will enter into that kingdom in their natural bodies with the power of procreation. The children born to these saints during the millennium will be in need of salvation, and this salvation will be brought to them through Israel.[19]

(7) Passages of scripture referring to the Second Coming must be divided into two categories: the rapture and the glorious appearing. We've already talked about this a little. When you read about the return of Christ in scripture, you must determine which phase of the Second Coming it's talking about—the rapture, or the glorious return to destroy the Antichrist.

In the pages to come, I would like to put this theory to the biblical test. There are a thousand different theories about Christ's return, but this one is so wildly popular that we need to step back from it and determine whether or not it has solid biblical support. If the theory is true, it will bear up under close examination.

Before we begin the examination, however, I would encourage you to visit the previous chapter one more time. Review the Bible passages we studied carefully. Then ask yourself this question: does the theory match what the scriptures say? Don't be too quick in your conclusions.

----

[16] Tim LaHaye and Jerry B. Jenkins, Are We Living in the Last Days? , p 100.

[17] Lindsey, Late Great Planet Earth, p. 132

[18] LaHaye, Popular Encyclopedia of Bible Prophecy, p. 236

[19] Ibid., p. 237.

CHAPTER SIX

Daniel's Stunning Prophecy

Daniel had grown old in captivity. His people still lived in Babylon, and the temple in Jerusalem still lay in ruins. He knew from the writings of the prophet Jeremiah that the time for restoration was drawing close, yet a vision had suggested to him that it would be a long time until the sanctuary was cleansed.[20]

To his way of thinking, it didn't add up. How could the captivity be nearly finished but the temple not restored for years to come? Eager to understand, Daniel began to fast and pray.[21]

His prayers were answered almost immediately. While he was still addressing God, the curtains of the heavenly realm were suddenly thrown open, and he received a visit from an angel. The information he acquired during that visit has, for centuries, silenced critics of the Bible, because of its stunning prophetic accuracy. It is easily one of the most remarkable prophecies of the Scriptures.

The angel's message is recorded in Daniel chapter nine. I have inserted verse numbers for easy reference:

(24) Seventy weeks are determined for your people and for your holy city, to finish the transgression, to make an end of sins, to make reconciliation for iniquity, to bring in everlasting righteousness, to seal up vision and prophecy, and to anoint the Most Holy.

(25) Know therefore and understand, that from the going forth of the command to restore and build Jerusalem until Messiah the Prince, there

shall be seven weeks and sixty-two weeks; the street shall be built again, and the wall, even in troublesome times.

(26) And after the sixty-two weeks Messiah shall be cut off, but not for Himself; and the people of the prince who is to come shall destroy the city and the sanctuary. The end of it shall be with a flood, and till the end of the war desolations are determined.

(27) Then he shall confirm a covenant with many for one week; but in the middle of the week he shall bring an end to sacrifice and offering. And on the wing of abominations shall be one who makes desolate, even until the consummation, which is determined, is poured out on the desolate. (Daniel 9:24-27)

This passage is known as the "seventy-week" prophecy of Daniel because of the reference to that period of time in the opening verse. Let's walk through it together carefully—because while it is one of the most striking prophecies in scripture, it is also one of the most widely misunderstood.

Just a quick word of caution before we begin: this chapter is going to get a little bit technical, and will require some math. Before you skip to the next chapter, I want to encourage you to stick with it. Study this material through several times, because it's essential to an understanding of Christ's return. It's not as complex as it might seem at first. Get out a pad of paper and take notes as you read. Draw the charts for yourself. A small investment of your time here will bring unbelievably rich dividends.

The angel Gabriel begins by informing Daniel that "seventy weeks" are determined for his people. Who are Daniel's people? The Jews. This prophecy sets aside a specific period of time for the nation of Israel.

In Bible prophecy, the language used to describe a period of time is usually symbolic. Generally speaking, a *day* is used in prophecy to represent a year.[22] Seventy weeks, or 490 days (70 weeks x 7 days a week = 490 days), is a period of 490 literal years. The period of time set aside for the nation of Israel is thus 490 years:

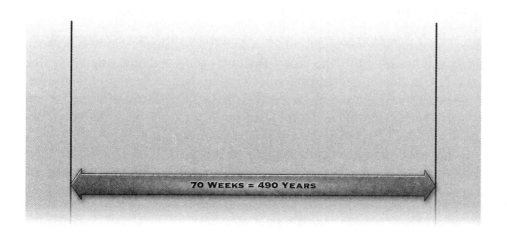

On its own, this information is of little value, because we have no idea when this period of time starts and when it ends. Fortunately, Gabriel provides a few more details that help us determine when this period begins and ends:

"...from the going forth of the command to restore and build Jerusalem until Messiah the Prince, there shall be seven weeks and sixty-two weeks..." (Daniel 9:25)

Daniel is told that there will be a total of 69 weeks (7 weeks + 62 weeks = 69 weeks) from the time that a decree is given to rebuild the city of Jerusalem until the Messiah appears. Using the day-for-a-year principle, we discover that this is a period of 483 years. (69 weeks x 7 days a week = 483 prophetic days, or literal years.)

There were four decrees given by Persian kings after the fall of Babylon for the Israelites to go back to their land and rebuild the city of Jerusalem. The first two decrees, both recorded in the Old Testament book of Ezra, were given in the years 537 B.C. and 520 B.C. respectively, but failed to accomplish anything significant. The third decree, given by Artaxerxes in 457 B.C. (also recorded in the book of Ezra), made the rebuilding of Jerusalem a reality. Not only did Artaxerxes make a decree, he also helped finance the project! (See Ezra 7:11-26.)

The decree was given in 457 B.C.; this, therefore becomes the starting point for the prophecy. Gabriel promised Daniel that 483 years after the decree, the Messiah would appear. That takes us to the year 27 A.D. (If you're doing the math yourself, you will discover that when you add 483 years to the date 457 B.C., you come to *26* A.D. not 27. Why does the prophecy terminate in 27 A.D.? It's because there was no such thing as a "year zero". The year 1 B.C. was followed immediately by the year 1 A.D. The math simply isn't done the way it normally would be, when you add years and cross the B.C./A.D. line. Because of the lack of a "zero" year, you must add one year to your total every time you cross the B.C./A.D. line. (See Appendix One for more details.)

Did anything significant happen in the year 27 A.D.? Absolutely! According to Luke 3:1, Jesus was baptized in the "fifteenth year of the reign of Tiberius Caesar," which was 27 A.D. At the Jordan River, God the Father publicly announced Jesus as His Son, and the Holy Spirit descended on Him (Luke 3:22). Luke 3:23 tells us specifically that immediately after His baptism Jesus began His public ministry.[23]

As a boy, I used to wonder why Jesus spent the first years of His life in relative obscurity. Why all those years of silence? I have often heard it explained that Christ waited until He was thirty years of age because that was the age of full majority in Jewish society. That made a lot of sense to me at the time, but now I think there's more to it than that. Jesus' ministry

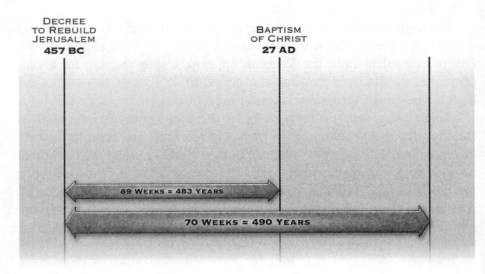

DECREE
TO REBUILD
JERUSALEM
457 BC

BAPTISM
OF CHRIST
27 AD

69 WEEKS = 483 YEARS

70 WEEKS = 490 YEARS

as Messiah would not begin until the 483 years of Daniel's prophecy had come to pass!

Given the remarkable accuracy of the prophecy, it is incomprehensible that the religious leaders of Jesus' day didn't have at least a sneaking suspicion that He really *was* the Messiah.

So, what does this prophecy have to do with the Second Coming of Christ? Everything. Gabriel has walked Daniel through the first 483 years (or 69 weeks) of the prophecy. There are seven years left over, or *one final week*. What happens during this time? Verse 26 adds some important details:

And after the sixty-two weeks Messiah shall be cut off, but not for Himself. (Daniel 9:26)

You'll remember that the 69 weeks in verse 25 were described as "seven weeks and sixty-two weeks." (I warned you that there would be a lot of math in this chapter!) There's an important reason that this time period is divided the way it is. Seven weeks would be 49 years, ending in 408 B.C. This was the year that the rebuilding of Jerusalem was completed. The first 49 years were a period of rebuilding, and the next 62 weeks (or 434 years) was a period in which Israel was waiting for the Messiah:

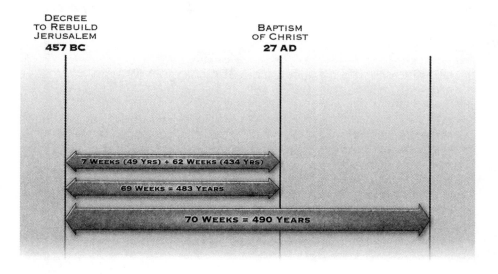

The sixty-two weeks end in 27 A.D., with the appearance of the Messiah. Gabriel tells us that *after* the sixty-two week period of time, Messiah would be "cut off," but not for Himself. This happened when Jesus was crucified in the spring of 31 A.D., after three and a half years of public ministry.

There is a second reference to the crucifixion in this prophecy, found in verse 27:

Then he shall confirm a covenant with many for one week; but in the middle of the week He shall bring an end to sacrifice and offering. (Daniel 9:27)

This is one of the most critical verses in the entire prophecy. Christ would confirm a covenant for "one week"—which is the period of time left over after the first 69 weeks came to a close in 27AD. In the "middle" of the week, He would put an end to sacrifices and offerings.

The death of Christ at Calvary put an end to the sacrificial system, which had sacrificed countless lambs in anticipation of the arrival of a "Lamb of God, who takes away the sin of the world" (John 1:29). Once Christ died for us at the cross, the sacrificial lambs that pointed to Him were no longer necessary. His crucifixion brought an end to "sacrifice and offering."

Amazingly, the crucifixion took place after three and a half years of ministry, *exactly in the middle of the last week of Daniel's prophecy:*

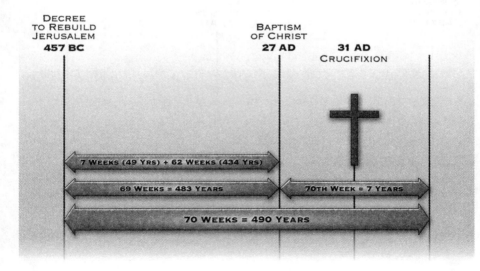

The obvious question, however, is this: if Christ died after three and a half years, how could He be said to have confirmed a covenant for one week, or a period of seven years? The answer is simple. Don't forget that the entire period of 490 years was set-aside for Daniel's people, the Jews (Daniel 9:24). Christ's disciples continued to minister to the nation of Israel for another three and a half years after He died, sharing the good news of the gospel in the temple and synagogues. Their additional three-and-a-half year ministry completes the prophecy, and the 70th week comes to its conclusion in 34 A.D.

Did anything significant happen in 34 A.D.? Yes. That year, the religious authorities of Israel stoned a deacon named Stephen to death. In the seventh chapter of the book of Acts Stephen preaches a final message of mercy to the leaders of Israel, recounting how God had painstakingly worked with their nation through the ages. At the close of Stephen's sermon, the outraged rulers put him to death. The Christian church was subsequently threatened with intense persecution by a young man named Saul, who had been present at Stephen's execution. As a result of his devastating campaign against the early church, many Christians were forced to scatter all over the known world.

As these Christians relocated, they also carried the gospel to the Gentile world, starting with Samaria (Acts 8:5). Precisely as predicted by Gabriel, the 490 years allotted to the nation of Israel had come to a close, and the gospel went beyond its borders. The covenant was thus confirmed with the nation of Israel for one final week through the ministry of both Jesus and His disciples.

The complete prophecy, remarkable for its breathtaking precision, looks like this: (see diagram on next page)

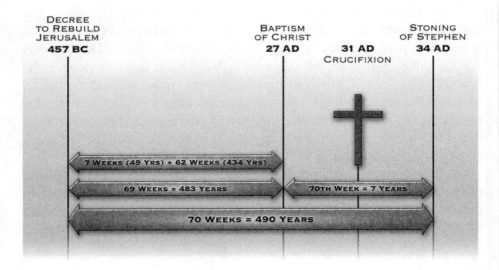

It is at this point that we have to ask some testing questions. The most popular theory about last-day events moves the final week of this prophecy to the end of the world. It is said to take place between two phases of Christ's coming, even though it seems most appropriate to leave it where it is, right after the first 69 weeks. Does that really make sense?

The Hard Questions

Let's suppose I give you directions to my house. "Drive down the freeway 70 miles," I tell you, "and then you'll see an exit that leads to my neighborhood."

With a 65 mph speed limit, you calculate that it will take just over an hour to reach the exit from your starting point. After driving for six hours, however, you still haven't seen it! You pull out your cell phone and call my house, frustrated.

"I've been driving for six hours, and I still don't see the exit you told me about! Didn't you tell me that it was about 70 miles?"

"Absolutely," I answer. "But what I didn't tell you was that between the sixty-ninth mile and the seventieth mile, there's a stretch of 2,000 miles!"

Would that make sense to you? Of course not. You'd expect that the seventieth mile would come right after the sixty-ninth, and you'd be right!

God is no less clear. When He tells us that the prophecy will last 70 weeks, or 490 years, He means exactly what He says. There is nothing in the ninth chapter of Daniel that even remotely suggests that we should insert a gap of nearly 2,000 years between the sixty-ninth and seventieth weeks—*yet this is precisely what modern expositors of prophecy are doing.*

Furthermore, the most popular theory in circulation today suggests that it is the *Antichrist* who confirms a covenant during the last week of the prophecy rather than Jesus. After the church has been raptured, the Antichrist is supposed to make a covenant with the nation of Israel. After three and a half years, he breaks his covenant and desecrates the newly built temple in Jerusalem.

In order for this to work, however, you have to assume that the first half of verse 26 is speaking of Jesus (the reference to "Messiah" makes it obvious), and the rest of the prophecy is speaking about the Antichrist. Here's how it needs to be divided up in order for it to work (the passage beginning with an [M] referring to the Messiah, and the passage beginning with an [A] referring to the Antichrist:

[M] *And after the sixty-two weeks Messiah shall be cut off, but not for Himself;* [A] *and the people of the prince who is to come shall destroy the city and the sanctuary. The end of it shall be with a flood, and till the end of the war desolations are determined. Then he shall confirm a covenant with many for one week; but in the middle of the week he shall bring an end to sacrifice and offering. And on the wing of abominations shall be one who makes desolate, even until the consummation, which is determined, is poured out on the desolate. (Daniel 9:26, 27)*

This *could* work, if it were assumed that the final week is somehow detached from the rest of the prophecy. Personally, it makes me very uncomfortable, because there is no indication whatsoever that we should divide the prophecy up that way. Is there an alternative?

The answer is *yes*. The Bible was not written in exactly the same manner in which modern people think. Our thought is usually in a strictly linear pattern, where each subject has a beginning, middle and a conclusion. The writers of the Bible, however, who were not members of modern Western Civilization, employ a number of literary devices, such as *chiasms*[24] and *parallel passages,* that were more in keeping with the way they thought.

A parallel passage alternates between two different subjects. It mentions subject "A" and then subject "B", and then it does it again. The structure of a passage written this way looks like this:

A—B—A—B, etc.

The final two verses of the prophecy are presented in this very format. It speaks alternately of the Messiah and the Roman destruction of Jerusalem in 70 A.D. (This makes perfect sense in light of the fact that the whole prophecy delineates the time left for the Jewish nation. Remember, Gabriel said that seventy weeks were determined for Daniel's people.)

The destruction of the temple sealed the fact that the time of probation set aside for the nation of Israel had long past. It should be noted that just prior to the crucifixion, as He left the temple for the very last time, Jesus declared "your house is left to you desolate" (Matthew 23:38).

Read the passage one more time. This time, I'll mark it with **[M]** for "Messiah" and **[R]** for the Roman armies. Notice the parallel structure, and notice how clearly it suddenly reads:

[M] *And after the sixty-two weeks Messiah shall be cut off, but not for Himself;* **[R]** *and the people of the prince who is to come shall destroy the city and the sanctuary. The end of it shall be with a flood, and till the end of the war desolations are determined.* **[M]** *Then he shall confirm a covenant with many for one week; but in the middle of the week he shall bring an end to sacrifice and offering.* **[R]** *And on the wing of abominations shall be one who makes desolate, even until the consummation, which is determined, is poured out on the desolate.* (Daniel 9:26, 27)

In typical style for a Bible writer, the passage alternates between two subjects. When it speaks of the Messiah (the main subject of the prophecy), it tells us that Jesus would be cut off for others, and that He would put an end to the sacrificial system in the middle of the week. This happened exactly as predicted. When it speaks of the Romans, it tells us that a prince will come to destroy the city and the sanctuary. Titus, the general who led the siege, was indeed a prince; in fact, he eventually became the Roman Emperor.

You don't have to cut the prophecy into pieces or insert gaps of thousands of years to make sense of it. *It makes sense exactly as it reads.*

Without a final seven years at the end of history, however, what becomes of the theory of the two-phase coming of Christ? Keep reading.

---

[20] See the vision of Daniel chapter 8:13, 14.

[21] Daniel's moving prayer is recorded in Daniel 9:3-19

[22] This is only true of Bible prophecy. See Numbers 14:34 and Ezekiel 4:6 for clear examples. When the Bible refers to a day elsewhere, such as in the seven days of creation, it means a literal day.

[23] Luke 3:23 tells us that Jesus was "about thirty years of age" at His baptism. Wouldn't He have been only 27 years old in 27 A.D.? Actually, the practice of numbering our years from the birth of Christ didn't come into use for many years after the New Testament was written. We have simply made a mistake. Today we know that Christ was likely born in about 4BC, or even a little earlier. (We know this because Herod the Great was still alive when Christ was born, and he died that year.)

[24] A chiasm is a literary device in which points A, B, and C are made in order, and then made again in the reverse order: C, B, and then A. Much of the book of Revelation, interestingly, is presented in this style.

CHAPTER SEVEN

Caught By Surprise

There is an important word we discussed earlier in the book: *parousia*. If you recall, it means "arrival" or "presence." It's a word that is used when a king makes a public appearance. It is used quite often of the Second Coming:

For this we say to you by the word of the Lord, that we who are alive and remain until the coming **[parousia]** *of the Lord will by no means precede those who are asleep. (1 Thessalonians 4:15)*

It is almost universally believed by those who teach a two-phase coming of Christ that this passage, along with its surrounding verses, applies to the rapture of the church. In fact, 1 Thessalonians 4:13-18 is often considered the key passage of the theory.

This passage refers to the *parousia* of Jesus, and it clearly refers to a time when Jesus comes for His church. A passage in the book of James makes it obvious that the early Christian church was, indeed, waiting for the *parousia* of Jesus:

Therefore be patient, brethren, until the coming of the Lord. See how the farmer waits for the precious fruit of the earth, waiting patiently for it until it receives the early and latter rain. You also be patient. Establish your hearts, for the coming **[parousia]** *of the Lord is at hand. (James 5: 7, 8)*

The apostle Paul points out the same thing:

And may the Lord make you increase and abound in love to one another and to all, just as we do to you, so that He may establish your hearts blameless in holiness before our God and Father at the coming **[parousia]** *of our Lord Jesus Christ with all His saints. (1 Thessalonians 3:12, 13)*

There is no question that the New Testament church was waiting for the *parousia.* If the rapture of the church takes place at the *parousia,* however, it raises an important question: why does Paul indicate in his second letter to the same church that the parousia will destroy the Antichrist?

And then the lawless one will be revealed, whom the Lord will consume with the breath of His mouth and destroy with the brightness of His coming **[parousia]**. *(2 Thessalonians 2:8)*

The problem in reconciling these verses is substantial. In the popular last-days theory, the church is first raptured at the *parousia,* and then the Antichrist appears for a period of seven years. But in Paul's version of events, the rapture of the church *coincides with the destruction of the Antichrist.*

How is it possible that the Antichrist is destroyed by the rapture if he hasn't even made himself known yet?

It's a good question. To make matters more complicated, consider what Jesus says in His Olivet discourse (Matthew 24). This famous sermon clearly refers to the glorious coming of Christ, *after the tribulation:*

"Immediately after the tribulation of those days the sun will be darkened, and the moon will not give its light; the stars will fall from heaven, and the powers of the heavens will be shaken. Then the sign of the Son of Man will appear in heaven, and then all the tribes of the earth will mourn, and they will see the Son of Man coming on the clouds of heaven with power and great glory. And He will send His angels with a great sound of a trumpet, and they will gather together His elect from the four winds, from one end of heaven to the other." (Matthew 24:29-31)

Few people would argue the fact that this is speaking about the final glorious coming of Christ. The tribulation is over. Everyone sees Jesus coming with "power and great glory." There's just one catch however— Jesus tells us that He is speaking about His *parousia:*

For as the lightning comes from the east and flashes to the west, so also will the coming **[parousia]** *of the Son of Man be. (Matthew 24:27)*

It's enough to make your head spin. If the *parousia* is the rapture (1 Thessalonians 4:15), and it's the event that the church was waiting for (James 5:7, 8; 1 Thessalonians 3:13), how can it also be the final destruction of the Antichrist and the glorious appearing after the tribulation? It doesn't make any sense—*unless you consider the possibility that there is only one phase to Christ's coming.*

A number of fine Bible scholars have pointed out that there are essentially three key Greek words used to describe the Second Coming of Christ: *parousia, apokalypse, and epiphany.* All three words, to a greater or lesser extent, convey the same idea—when Jesus comes, it will be a public event.

Parousia, as we've already discovered, means "coming, arrival, presence." *Apokalypse* means, "to pull away the veil, a revealing." (The original Greek name for the book of Revelation, incidentally, is *apokalypse.* It is something that is revealed.) *Epiphany* is a "manifestation"—something that people see unfolding before their eyes.

All three words speak of something that is revealed, or made public. None of them refer to an event that is concealed, secret, or private. We have already looked at a number of passages that use the word *parousia.* Let me give you some examples of passages that use the other two words:

...even as the testimony of Christ was confirmed in you, so that you come short in no gift, eagerly waiting for the revelation **[apokalypse]** *of our Lord Jesus Christ. (1 Corinthians 1:6, 7)*

Beloved, do not think it strange concerning the fiery trial which is to try you, as though some strange thing happened to you; but rejoice to the extent that you partake of Christ's sufferings, that when His glory is revealed **[apokalypse]**, *you may also be glad with exceeding joy. (1 Peter 4:12, 13)*

In both of these passages, the Christian church is clearly waiting for the "revealing" of Jesus. According to Paul, the "revealing" of Jesus happens when God punishes the wicked:

...it is a righteous thing with God to repay with tribulation those who troubled you, and to give you who are troubled rest with us when the Lord Jesus is revealed **[apokalypse]** *from heaven with His mighty angels, in flaming fire taking vengeance on those who do not know*

God, and on those who do not obey the gospel of our Lord Jesus Christ.
(2 Thessalonians 1:6-8)

This is a powerful passage that helps clear the air on the subject of a two-phase coming of Christ. Paul tells us that the church will find rest at the *apokalypse* of Jesus. It is assumed by many that this happens at a "secret" rapture, but the rest of the passage describes events that would happen at the final glorious appearing of Christ. The church finds its rest at the same moment that the wicked are punished. (In other words, final rewards have already been decided when Christ comes.) In the two-phase theory of Christ's coming, the wicked would not notice Christ coming for His church. Here are a couple of passages that speak about the *epiphany* of Jesus:

Finally, there is laid up for me the crown of righteousness, which the Lord, the righteous judge, will give to me on that Day, and not to me only but also to all who have loved His appearing **[epiphany]**. *(2 Tim. 4:8)*

...looking for the blessed hope and glorious appearing **[epiphany]** *of our great God and Savior Jesus Christ... (Titus 2:13)*

In each of these passages, the church is looking for the *epiphany,* or "appearing" of Jesus. Again, it is assumed by many that the Christian community is waiting for the rapture of the church—the first phase of Christ's coming. In the second passage, however, we discover that the church is waiting for the *glorious* appearing of Christ.

When you line up all the passages that speak of the Second Coming of Christ, it becomes evident that the Bible speaks of only one event. *Christ comes for the church at the same time that He comes in glory.*

A Thief in the Night

Some have argued, however, that Luke 21, Mark 13 and Matthew 24 (three versions of the Olivet discourse) are addressed only to the children of Israel who will still be here during a final seven-year tribulation period. The belief is that, because the prophetic clock stopped at the cross, the church will not have any signs to watch for; Jesus could come at any moment. The Olivet discourse could not possibly be for them. After the rapture, however, the Jewish believers will have lots of signs to watch for; these prophecies are obviously for the Jews.

There is a serious problem with this understanding. First of all, the signs of the times listed in these chapters not only apply to the Second

Coming; they also apply to the destruction of the temple in 70 A.D. If the prophetic clock stopped with the beginning of the Christian era, why does Jesus waste time with an event that takes place nearly 40 years after His ascension? It is clear that the early church did indeed have prophetic signs to watch for!

Secondly, and most importantly, is the context provided by Matthew in his version of this prophecy. If the Olivet discourse is directed only at the Jewish believers of the last days, why does Jesus include a passage which is frequently quoted by proponents of the two-phase theory as pertaining to the rapture of the church?

"But of that day and hour no one knows, no not even the angels of heaven, but My Father only. But as the days of Noah were, so also will the coming of the Son of Man be. For as in the days before the flood, they were eating and drinking, marrying and giving in marriage, until the day that Noah entered the ark, and did not know until the flood came and took them all away, so also will the coming of the Son of Man be. Then two men will be in the field: one will be taken, and the other left. Two women will be grinding at the mill: one will be taken and the other left. Watch therefore, for you do not know what hour your Lord is coming." *(Matthew 24:36-42)*

Some people have insisted that this is a description of an imminent secret rapture of the church. Nobody knows when it will happen; there are no prophecies leading up to it. Some will mysteriously be raptured away, others will be left behind.

But if the Olivet discourse was only for last-day Jewish believers, why include a description of the rapture? As you read the whole passage carefully, it becomes abundantly clear that Jesus only spoke of *one* coming. In the very same sermon, He describes the Second Coming like this:

"Then the sign of the Son of Man will appear in heaven, and then all the tribes of the earth will mourn, and they will see the Son of Man coming on the clouds of heaven with power and great glory. And He will send His angels with a great sound of a trumpet, and they will gather together His elect from the four winds, from one end of heaven to the other." *(Matthew 24:30, 31)*

The church is gathered at the same moment the wicked mourn the coming of Christ. Jesus moves quickly from this description, which is clearly the *glorious* coming of Christ witnessed by everyone, into the famous passage about people being left behind. Jesus said nothing to make us assume that we're supposed to draw a distinction between the two events. They are one and the same.

Read the "left behind" passage one more time. It simply says that some are taken, and others are left behind. It says nothing at all about a secret coming of Christ, or a time when the world wonders where the Christians have gone. It simply says that some will be taken, and others left behind.

It also says that the Second Coming will be like the Flood. Verse 39 tells us that it was the *wicked* that were taken away in Noah's day—not the righteous. Noah and his family were *left behind*. The two-phase theory teaches that the *church* is taken, and the *wicked* are left behind— but this is not what the passage says. The truth is quite the opposite: when Jesus comes, the wicked are slain, and the righteous are left behind to inherit eternity with Christ.

There is a passage in Luke's gospel that makes this very clear:

"I tell you, in that night there will be two men in one bed: the one will be taken and the other will be left. Two women will be grinding together: the one will be taken and the other left. Two men will be in the field: the one will be taken and the other left."

And they answered and said to Him, "Where, Lord?" So He said to them, "Wherever the body is, there the eagles will be gathered together." (Luke 17:34-37)

Notice the disciples' question: Where will they be taken? Jesus' answer: They'll be left for the eagles.

Notice the description of the Second Coming found in the nineteenth chapter of Revelation:

Then I saw an angel standing in the sun; and he cried with a loud voice, saying to all the birds that fly in the midst of heaven, "Come and gather together for the supper of the Great God, that you may eat the flesh of kings, the flesh of captains, the flesh of mighty men, the flesh of horses and of those who sit on them, and the flesh of all people, free and slave, both small and great ....

And the rest were killed with the sword which proceeded from the mouth of Him who sat on the horse. And all the birds were filled with their flesh. (Revelation 19:17,18, 21)

When some are "taken," they are taken the same way the wicked were taken by the flood. They are destroyed. When some are "left," they are left to be with Jesus.

Christ's appearing will be a huge surprise to the wicked. The Bible says that it will sneak up on them like a "thief in the night." This is not because Christ comes *secretly*, but because they are caught off guard. Notice how the "left behind" passage ends in Matthew 24:

"Watch therefore, for you do not know what hour your Lord is coming. But know this, that if the master of the house had known what hour the thief would come, he would have watched and not allowed his house to be broken into. Therefore you also be ready, for the Son of Man is coming at an hour when you do not expect Him." (Matthew 24:42-44)

Those who perished in the flood were not unaware of what was happening. They were simply caught by surprise. They did not expect things to happen as Noah predicted. They were too caught up in the affairs of every day life to pay much attention. When the floodwaters arrived, it was too late.

Most nights, you go to bed quietly, never expecting a thief to break in. When you suddenly hear a window break or someone walking in the hallway, you are surprised—but you are not unaware that it is happening.

The same will be true for those who did not prepare for the Second Coming. Many have said that the return of Christ is compared to a "thief in the night" because it happens by stealth. Read the other "thief" passages of the Bible carefully—you'll discover that nothing is said about stealth:

But the day of the Lord will come as a thief in the night, in which the heavens will pass away with a great noise, and the elements will melt with fervent heat; both the earth and the works that are in it will be burned up. (2 Peter 3:10)

"Remember therefore how you have received and heard; hold fast and repent. Therefore if you will not watch, I will come upon you as a thief, and you will not know what hour I will come upon you." (Revelation 3:3)

"Behold, I am coming as a thief. Blessed is he who watches, and keeps his garments, lest he walk naked and they see his shame." (Revelation 16:15)

Jesus' appearing will come as a devastating surprise to those who are not ready. This is the message of the "thief." There will not be any second chances after Christ comes for His church.

Christians, on the other hand, while they do not know the precise timing of Christ's coming, will not be caught by surprise. They will be expecting it. It will not come as a thief for them!

CHAPTER EIGHT

Tribulation

It is almost universally believed—and with good biblical reason—
that there will be a period of great difficulty prior to the final coming
of Christ in glory. In the two-phase coming of Christ theory, this is
understood to take place after the church has been raptured. But since
there is actually only *one* phase to Christ's coming, this trying time must
take place while the church is still here.

Generally speaking, there are three key passages often quoted to
defend the idea that the church will be absent from the earth during
history's worst hour. Let's look at them one at a time:

(1) Revelation 3:10

*"Because you have kept My command to persevere, I also will keep
you from the hour of trial which shall come upon the whole world, to test
those who dwell on the earth." (Revelation 3:10)*

At first glance, it certainly seems that the church will be absent during
the "hour of trial which shall come upon the whole world." But let's ask
an honest question of the passage. Does it say Christ will *remove* His
church, or *keep* it?

The sixteenth chapter of Revelation describes seven terrible plagues
that will fall on the earth just prior to the second coming of Christ. They
are described as the "wrath of God." They are also described as the seven
last plagues (Revelation 15:1).

These are not the *only* plagues to fall on planet earth—they are simply the *last* ones. If you read the context carefully, you'll notice that before John sees the plagues in detail, he is shown God's people immediately after they have passed through a terrible trial:

Then I saw another sign in heaven, great and marvelous: seven angels having the seven last plagues, for in them the wrath of God is complete. And I saw something like a sea of glass mingled with fire, and those who have the victory over the beast, over his image and over his mark and over the number of his name, standing on the sea of glass, having harps of God. And they sing the song of Moses, the servant of God, and the song of the Lamb.... (Revelation 15:1-3)

It is important to remember that most of the imagery used in the book of Revelation is borrowed or quoted from other parts of the Bible. Some scholars have estimated that as much as two thirds of the book is borrowed from the rest of scripture. This is especially true of the fifteenth and sixteenth chapters of the book of Revelation, which to a large extent use the experience of ancient Israel's exodus from Egypt to describe the final deliverance of God's people.

Look at the language carefully. There are plagues falling on the planet, just as there were plagues that fell on Egypt prior to the Exodus. God's people are shown singing the "song of Moses" on the "sea," just as ancient Israel sang the song of Moses on the far side of the Red Sea after their deliverance from the Egyptian army. The parallels are quite clear.

During the ancient plagues that fell on Egypt, Israel was not removed from the land until after the plagues had fallen. They remained in the land of Goshen, completely sheltered from the last seven of the ten plagues! (See Exodus 7-12.)[25]

Take that information and apply it to the prophecies of Revelation 15 and 16, and it sheds new light on the subject. In the last days, just before Jesus comes, there will be a repeat of the experience of ancient Israel. God's wrath against sin, in the form of plagues, will fall on the entire planet—and, just like ancient Israel, the church will be present for those plagues. They will be *kept* from them, however, as promised in the ninety-first Psalm:

Surely He shall deliver you from the snare of the fowler
And from the perilous pestilence.
He shall cover you with His feathers,

And under His wings you shall take refuge;
His truth shall be your shield and buckler.
You shall not be afraid of the terror by night,
Nor of the arrow that flies by day,
Nor of the pestilence that walks in darkness,
Nor of the destruction that lays waste at noonday.
A thousand may fall at your side,
And ten thousand at your right hand;
But it shall not come near you.
Only with your eyes shall you look,
And see the reward of the wicked.
Because you have made the Lord,
who is my refuge,
Even the Most High, your habitation,
No evil shall befall you,
Nor shall any plague come near your dwelling;
For He shall give His angels charge over you,
To keep you in all your ways.
(Psalm 91:3-11)

There is nothing in scripture to suggest that we will not be here as the plagues begin to fall. We *will* be here, and we will be sheltered from the effects of the wrath of God. At the end of the plagues, we will finally stand victorious on the sea of crystal, singing the song of Moses and the Lamb. We will sing the song of deliverance.

(2) 1 Thessalonians 5:9

For God did not appoint us to wrath, but to obtain salvation through our Lord Jesus Christ. (1 Thessalonians 5:9)

In light of our discussion of the final plagues, this passage becomes quite clear. The wrath of God is poured out on the earth just prior to the return of Christ, but the Christian church is sheltered from it. God's wrath is not directed at us.

There is a broader context to this passage as well. The primary subject is our *salvation*. Paul is emphasizing what Jesus has already told us about the choice we have between salvation and condemnation:

"For God so loved the world that He gave His only begotten Son, that whoever believes in Him should not perish but have everlasting life.

For God did not send His Son into the world to condemn the world, but that the world through Him might be saved. He who believes in Him is not condemned; but he who does not believe is condemned already, because he has not believed in the name of the only begotten Son of God." (John 3:16-18)

Then John adds:

He who believes in the Son has everlasting life; and he who does not believe the Son shall not see life, but the wrath of God abides on him. (John 3:36)

The primary issue in 1 Thessalonians 5:9 and John 3:36 is not the final time of trouble; rather, a person's final decision for or against Christ. Those who are in Christ will be rewarded with eternal life, but those who are not will be appointed to wrath. Paul adds the following detail to this subject in his letter to the Romans:

Or do you despise the riches of His goodness, forbearance, and longsuffering, not knowing that the goodness of God leads you to repentance? But in accordance with your hardness and your impenitent heart you are treasuring up for yourself wrath in the day of wrath and revelation of the righteous judgment of God, who will render to each one according to his deeds: eternal life to those who by patient continuance in doing good seek for glory, honor and immortality; but to those who are self-seeking and do not obey the truth, but obey unrighteousness—indignation and wrath, tribulation and anguish, on every soul of man who does evil, of the Jew first and also of the Greek; but glory, honor and peace to everyone who works what is good, to the Jew first and also to the Greek. (Romans 2:4-10)

Because of the cross of Calvary, genuine Christians will never experience the wrath of God. Christ suffered God's wrath against sin in our place. Through the shedding of His blood, we have been appointed to salvation instead.

Christians have not been spared, however, from going through a period of tribulation. There is nothing in 1 Thessalonians 5:9 to suggest that the church will be absent. If you read the passage in context, Paul is simply pointing out what happens *after Christ comes.* He is speaking of our reward, suggesting that the wicked "shall not escape," (1 Thessalonians 5:3) and that those who serve Him will be delivered from the "wrath to come" (1 Thessalonians 1:9, 10).

(3) Luke 21:36

"Watch, therefore, and pray always that you may be counted worthy to escape all these things that will come to pass, and to stand before the Son of Man." (Luke 21:36)

It has been suggested that this passage teaches that Jesus will rapture the church away before the signs He speaks of come to pass. Christians, therefore, will not see them. A simple glance at the context, however, sets the record straight:

"And there will be signs in the sun, in the moon, and in the stars; and on the earth distress of nations, with perplexity, the sea and the waves roaring; men's hearts failing them from fear and the expectation of those things which are coming on the earth, for the powers of heaven will be shaken. Then they will see the Son of Man coming in a cloud with power and great glory. Now when these things begin to happen, look up and lift up your heads, because your redemption draws near." (Luke 21:25-28)

There is no doubt that Christians will escape the plagues and the final wrath of God. That much is promised in scripture. There is nothing to suggest, however, that *we will be absent* during earth's final moments. In fact, Jesus plainly tells us that when we see these things begin to happen, we'll know it's nearly time for our final deliverance.

As things get rough on planet earth, God's people will suddenly find deliverance as Christ returns in glory.

As you glance through scripture, you quickly discover that nowhere does it suggest that God's church will avoid trials or tribulations. Noah and his family were saved from the flood, but *they still went through it*. The Israelites were spared the last seven plagues, but *they still went through them*. The early Christian church suffered severe persecution by the Roman Empire, but God carried them through it. Stalwart Christian believers of the Dark Ages, like the Waldenses, suffered terrible things at the hands of persecutors, but the church survived and triumphed. Likewise, the last-day Christian church will also triumph, but we will *still go through a time of trouble*.

Take another look at the passage from 1 Peter 4 that we quoted earlier. Peter tells us, point blank, that our suffering continues until the glorious return of Jesus Christ:

Beloved, do not think it strange concerning the fiery trial which is to try you, as though some strange thing happened to you; but rejoice to

the extent that you partake of Christ's sufferings, that when His glory is
revealed, you may also be glad with exceeding joy. 1 Peter 4:12, 13

There is nothing in the Bible to suggest that our hope during the last
days should be any different.

---

25 It appears that the first three plagues—bloody water, frogs, and lice—may have
been common to both the Israelites and the Egyptians.

CHAPTER NINE

Antichrist

It was a small light-brown book—the sort you'd find in a free literature rack. A bit dog-eared, it had obviously been read through a few times. I found it lying on the small table beside my grandfather's chair, picked it up and thumbed through it. The book was so short I was able to read it from beginning to end in just a few minutes. What it lacked in length, however, was made up by the content.

Just imagine, I thought to myself after paging through it a second time. *All of the world's Christians could disappear at any given moment—all of them!* I stole a glance out the window up at the sky to see if there were any detectable signs of Christ's coming. Of course, there were none.

I have no idea what became of that little book, but I still remember it vividly. The descriptions of empty cars careening off the freeway were spellbinding. The thought that you might wake up one morning to discover that your entire family had been taken to heaven without you was frightening.

That little dog-eared book was one of the things that started my life-long love for the prophecies of the Bible. I say "one of the things," because in reality, it was the Bible itself that sparked my love for the subject. At the age of six, my parents bought me my first Bible. I probably spent more time engrossed in the mysterious symbols of Revelation than in any other section. Once in a while, I would go out to the back yard, look up at the sky, and try to imagine what it will be like when Jesus finally comes back. I had only a handful of verses tucked away in my boyhood memory to go on, but I knew that when Jesus returned, every eye would see Him.

The author of the little brown book, however, seemed to disagree. He said that when Jesus came, only some people would see Him—at least during the first phase of His coming. The Christians would be well aware that Jesus had come, as they were with Him, but the rest of the world—after adjusting to the shock of millions of missing people—would go about its regular day-to-day business.

It was a little different than I had been led to believe by reading the Bible for myself, but the author seemed very knowledgeable, and I knew him to be a fine Christian. Maybe there was more to the Second Coming than I originally thought!

A number of other seemingly trustworthy sources appeared to confirm what the little brown book said. At the Bible camp I attended as a boy, sometimes they would show films that usually began with some poor soul waking up to discover that his wife had been taken to heaven while he was sleeping. Books like *The Late Great Planet Earth* said the same thing.

Well, I thought, *there must be something to this.*

I did not grow up in a church tradition that taught the two-phase coming of Christ, but because of constant exposure to it, I came to adopt the theory as my own. I wasn't adamant about it—it just seemed to be the way that a lot of Christians were reading their Bibles. Who was I to argue?

Over time, however, I developed a growing sense of discomfort with the theory, because I couldn't find anything in the scriptures that actually said that Christ's return would be a two-part act. The passage quoted most often to defend the idea was 1 Thessalonians 4:13-18, where Jesus returns to raise the righteous dead; but I had trouble seeing how in the world an event like that could take place quietly behind the scenes while the unbelieving world didn't notice. It seemed it would be such a catastrophic, noisy event that it couldn't possibly be a secret. It didn't make sense.

Over the years, a growing number of people have added their voices to a swelling chorus of honest questions. If this theory is in the Bible, why is it so hard to find? Why is there not a single passage that describes a two-part coming of Jesus, with an initial secret coming and a secondary glorious coming?

And if the theory is not to be found in the Bible, why is it so popular? Where did it come from? Could so many sincere Christians really be mistaken about something as important or as central to the scriptures as the Second Coming of Christ?

If the *first* coming of Christ is any indication, the answer is a resounding *yes*. One of the reasons that so many people had trouble accepting Jesus as the Messiah is that their expectations were wrong. They had confused the prophecies of Jesus' birth and His second coming. They were expecting Him to establish His physical kingdom right away. Their fondest hope, of course, was that the Messiah would put an end to Roman rule and re-establish Israel as a kingdom in its own right— something that hadn't actually been a reality since before the Babylonian captivity. What they had failed to notice, however, was the considerable list of prophecies that pointed to His death, burial and resurrection.

The cross simply didn't fit into their plans.

Even John the Baptist—named by Jesus as the greatest of all prophets (Matthew 11:11)—failed to interpret the prophecies correctly. After his arrest by Herod, John became a little concerned that Jesus had done nothing to establish His kingdom and set him free:

Now it came to pass, when Jesus finished commanding His twelve disciples, that He departed from there to teach and to preach in their cities. And when John had heard in prison about the works of Christ, he sent two of his disciples and said to Him, "Are You the Coming One, or do we look for another?" (Matthew 11:1-3)

If John the Baptist, who was handpicked by God to herald the coming of Christ, could be wrong, is it possible that we could be wrong, too? Nobody questions the sincerity of John, and I don't question the sincerity of the author of the little brown book. But I've been forced to come to the conclusion that the two-phase theory of Christ's coming is mistaken.

When I investigated *where* the theory came from, I made a rather interesting discovery.

The Protestant Reformation of the sixteenth century completely altered the face of Christianity. First of all, it brought about much-needed reforms for the clergy of the day. Secondly, it challenged people to return to an honest reading of the Word of God, and it restored the Scriptures to their rightful place in the Christian community.

Additionally, the Reformation raised the subject of Bible prophecy in a very unusual way. As the movement spread across Europe, most of the Reformers identified the papal system of church government as the Antichrist of Bible prophecy. They were able to come to this conclusion because up to this point, the overwhelming majority of Bible students followed something known as the *historical* method of understanding Bible prophecy.

The historical method, or *historicism*, simply teaches that the major prophecies of the Bible were meant to be understood as unfolding in a long chain of events that stretches from the time the prophecy was given until the return of Christ.

A great example of the historical method can be seen in Nebuchadnezzar's dream. The image, made of four metals and clay, was a portrayal of successive kingdoms from the time of Babylon through to the establishment of Christ's kingdom. It was an uninterrupted chain of events that stretched through all of earth's history.

In the *historicist* method of interpreting prophecy, the seven churches of the book of Revelation are seen as seven periods of church history stretching from the establishment of the New Testament church (the church of Ephesus) to the moment just before Jesus comes (the church of Laodicea). (This is still the understanding of the vast majority of Bible scholars to this day. It is only the later passages of Revelation that are understood differently.)

For nearly two thousand years of Christian history, the appearance of the Antichrist was expected to occur some time in the course of history, after the collapse of the Roman Empire, and *before* Jesus came for His church. This is quite different from the two-phase theory, which teaches that the Antichrist will appear *after* Jesus comes for His church.

A close examination of the scriptures reveals that the scholars of yesteryear were quite right. The church in Thessalonica had become very excited by Paul's first letter, which described the Second Coming so vividly. Apparently, they got a little *too* excited and expected Jesus to come at any moment. In Paul's second letter to the Thessalonians, he deals a deathblow to the idea that Jesus' coming was imminent. He points out something the church was supposed to watch for:

Now, brethren, concerning the coming of our Lord Jesus Christ and our gathering together to Him, we ask you, not to be soon shaken in mind or troubled, either by spirit or by word or by letter, as if from us, as though the day of Christ had come. Let no one deceive you by any means; for that Day will not come unless the falling away comes first, and the man of sin is revealed, the son of perdition, who opposes and exalts himself above all that is called God or that is worshiped, so that he sits as God in the temple of God, showing himself that he is God. (2 Thessalonians 2:1-4)

Paul couldn't be clearer: the Antichrist will be revealed *before* Jesus comes again! And lest someone should argue that this prophecy was for those who were "left behind" at Christ's secret coming, let's not forget who his audience is. It's a Christian church that existed nearly 2,000 years ago! The Thessalonians were waiting for Christ to come *for them*, and Paul says it will not happen until after the Antichrist appears.

The natural question, of course, is this: if Paul is so crystal clear, how in the world did we get so mixed up? Why is it that so many Christians believe that Christ will come for them *before* the Antichrist is revealed?

Let's go back to the Protestant Reformation. Knowing full well that the Antichrist would appear before Christ returned, and able to point to the rampant corruption in the organized church of the day, Bible scholars (including some notable Catholic scholars) saw a fulfillment of Bible prophecy in the papal organization. As this understanding spread, needless to say, it made life a little uncomfortable for Rome. The authorities of the church recognized that a growing number of fingers were pointing directly at the Vatican, and they felt a growing need to direct attention elsewhere.

A number of Jesuit scholars, known for their zealous defense of Rome, were commissioned to come up with an alternate interpretation of Bible prophecy. This resulted in two new theories, both of which diverted the finger of Bible prophecy elsewhere. The two theories are called *preterism* and *futurism*.

Preterism was the brainchild of a scholar by the name of Luis Alcazar. In his theory, which is still taught in some circles today, the book of Revelation was written primarily for the early New Testament church as it braced itself against the persecutions of pagan Rome. Most of the prophecies, therefore, only apply to the first few generations of

Christians, and the Antichrist is the Emperor Nero—someone who existed before the establishment of the papal system.

Futurism was by far the more successful theory. Pioneered by Cardinal Robert Bellarmine and Dr. Francisco Ribera it taught that most of Bible prophecy will be fulfilled some time in the distant future. The first few chapters of the Revelation were for the church of the New Testament, but the rest of the book is supposed to apply to a three-and-a-half-year period of time in which the Antichrist would conduct a reign of terror on earth. This interpretation, of course, exempted the papal system from being identified by prophecy at all—and forms the foundation for the two-phase theory of Christ's coming! Joseph Tanner elaborates on what happened:

> Accordingly, towards the close of the century of the Reformation, two of her most learned doctors set themselves to the task, each endeavouring by different means to accomplish the same end, namely, that of diverting men's minds from perceiving the fulfillment of the prophecies of the Antichrist in the Papal system. The Jesuit Alcasar devoted himself to bring into prominence the *Preterist* method of interpretation, which we have already briefly noticed, and thus endeavoured to show that the prophecies of Antichrist were fulfilled before the Popes ever ruled at Rome, and therefore could not apply to the Papacy. On the other hand the Jesuit Ribera tried to set aside the application of these prophecies to the Papal Power by bringing out the *Futurist* system, which asserts that these prophecies refer properly not to the career of the Papacy, but to that of some future supernatural individual, who is yet to appear, and to continue in power for three and a half years. Thus, as Alford says, the Jesuit Ribera, about A.D. 1580, may be regarded as the founder of the Futurist system in modern times.[26]

Unwittingly, modern futurism, which teaches the two-phase theory, has adopted Ribera's system almost wholesale—and it's a system that was deliberately manufactured to take sixteenth century eyes off of Rome. In the last 200 years or so, this theory, which was created as a political maneuver, has made tremendous headway in evangelical Christian circles.

One large problem that emerges almost immediately when considering this theory is the fact that nearly two thousand years of Christian history are suddenly not accounted for. If the prophetic clock stopped at the cross, and will not start again until after the rapture of the church, what do we do with the 2,000 years—roughly one third of earth's history—that fall between those events? Is that incredible span of time not included in the Bible narrative, when the rest of recorded history is?

The explanation offered is that the Old Testament prophets simply couldn't see the Christian era. Just as when you look at a mountain range, you can't see the valleys in between, it is assumed that the prophets could see the peaks (the cross, the tribulation, the Antichrist, the glorious return of Christ), but not the valleys in between (the Christian era). The following drawing based on an old diagram from noted illustrator Clarence Larkin demonstrates this point of view:

It's an interesting theory, but it suffers from one notable deficiency. *It has absolutely no biblical support.* For example, we've already seen that Paul predicted the appearance of the Antichrist while the church was still here on earth. Nebuchadnezzar's dream forecast the Roman Empire and its breakup into ten pieces in 476 A.D., which occurred well into the church age.

This futurist theory simply doesn't make any sense. Why would God take such care to record the history of the New Testament church in the Bible, but give it no mention at all in Bible prophecy? The Christian church, which is the "body" of God's own Son, is treated almost as an afterthought—a "plan B" that God resorted to when "plan A" with the Jews didn't work out.

The only sense it makes, really, is to divert your attention away from anything that might happen during the church age—*which is exactly why the theory was first created.* It has an entire generation of believers not expecting the Antichrist in their lifetime, which makes them good candidates for the religious deceptions the Antichrist brings with him. After all, it couldn't possibly be the Antichrist, because he's not supposed to be here yet, right?

---

[26] Joseph Tanner, Daniel and the Revelation, pp. 16,17 in Froom, Prophetic Faith of Our Fathers, Vol 2, p. 487.

CHAPTER TEN

A Tale of Two Cities

The two-phase coming of Christ may be a very popular theory, but it's also a relatively recent one. You will search in vain for any reference to it in Christian writing, either Protestant or Catholic, before the counter-reformation of the sixteenth century. In Protestant circles, it didn't make any real headway until the late eighteenth century.

Margaret MacDonald was a very sick young lady—so sick, in fact, that it was generally assumed that she was going to die. She made her home in Port Glasgow, Scotland, where in the year 1830 she had an experience that would change her life. She claimed she had a vision:

Throughout the morning I had felt very unwell, and disinclined to converse with any one; so much so that when Mrs. _____ called as usual to inquire for me, I wished not to see her, and told her I was not able to talk with her, but she might pray. A few verses of the 106th Psalm were sung: while singing that part of it "His tender mercy doth endure," etc. I was quite overpowered with a sense of the presence of God, and constrained to cry out, "Eternity, eternity will never unfold its depth." Immediately I was so swallowed up in God I did not see those who were with me in the room, nor hear their voices singing, but I heard the trump of God sounding in my ears so loud that all other sounds were lost. Indeed I heard unutterable things: the sound of the trumpet seemed to wax louder and louder as if that moment the Lord was to have been revealed. I felt surrounded by the heavenly hosts, a multitude which no man could number, and heard them singing, "Alleluia, for the Lord God omnipotent reigneth." Oh, it was a blessed sound, and I felt constrained to join with them, and sing loudly the same glorious song. I did not feel on this earth—I thought it had vanished at the presence of the Lord. In spirit I saw the Lord coming in the glory of his Father and of all the holy angels, so that I was quite swallowed up in transport. I thought I had just to open my eyes and see the King in his beauty. No language can express the glorious things which were made to pass before me....[27]

This would not be the last vision that Miss MacDonald would experience. Naturally, family and friends were hesitant about this supposed manifestation of the Spirit, but further episodes convinced them. The visions seemed in perfect keeping with the dramatic religious revival that was sweeping the nation at the time. Before long, churches and prayer meetings around the Scottish countryside were discussing the prophetic insights of a sickly young lady who, apparently, had heard from God.

In time, a new and peculiar view of the Second Coming surfaced in the discussions that Margaret had with people. She began to speak about a time when the church would be taken away so that it would not have to experience the tribulation. A letter written by an acquaintance of Margaret's to his sister expresses this sentiment:

...the Lord is nigh, even at the door. It is because there is no safety where you are, because you cannot be sealed where you are, it is because if you are not sealed you must be left in the tribulations, while those who have obeyed His voice shall be caught up to meet Him.[28]

When the famous preacher, John Darby (of the Brethren) heard about the revival in Scotland, he decided to investigate. In 1830, he traveled to the region and, among other things, made contact with Margaret. His written records indicate that he was unimpressed with her gift, and go into considerable detail regarding what transpired during the visit.[29]

As author Dave MacPherson points out, however, something remarkable is missing from Darby's account of his visit. Not once does he mention Miss MacDonald's teaching on the Second Coming, even though it had become such a central part of her teaching. Interestingly, Darby himself came out with a two-phase Second Coming theory at about the same time—and his version has proliferated throughout the evangelical world!

Is it possible that John Darby didn't mention Margaret's theory because he plagiarized the idea from her? Many have said he did, and point to the fact that he was highly intolerant of other prophecy teachers of the day. Admittedly, it looks a little fishy—but let's give Darby the benefit of the doubt for a minute. Let's suppose that he came up with a similar theory by sheer coincidence. That still leaves a rather significant problem: the two-phase theory doesn't make an appearance in mainstream Christianity until 1,800 years after Christ!

Staunch defenders of the two-phase theory have pointed out that it made an appearance in Christianity prior to 1830:

> For several years opponents of the pre-Trib position have argued that it was invented by John Darby in the mid-1800s and was never mentioned before that. Quite simply, this argument is false—a fact that cost one post-Trib writer a bundle of cash. This author offered five hundred dollars to anyone who could prove that the pre-Trib Rapture theory was known before John Darby began to popularize it in the 1840s. When it was discovered that the Reverend Morgan Edwards saw it back in 1742, the writer had to pay off his costly challenge. He has since had to admit his error and withdraw his offer.
>
> The Reverend Morgan Edwards was a Baptist pastor in Philadelphia who described a pre-Trib return of Christ for His church in his 1788 book, *Millennium, Last Days Novelties*. Although he saw only a three-and-a-half year Tribulation, he definitely saw the Rapture occur before that Tribulation. What is even more interesting is that he claimed he had preached and written the same thing as early as 1742. He may have been influenced by John Gill before him or by others whose writings or teachings were available at that time but have not been preserved.[30]

Personally, I have to admit that if what this writer says is true, then Margaret MacDonald cannot possibly be considered the originator of the pre-Tribulation rapture theory. Yet, it doesn't solve the problem of time, because you still have a 1,700-year gap between the writing of the New Testament and the entrance of the two-phase theory into mainline Christianity.

It's important to notice that all of these people—Margaret MacDonald, John Darby, and Morgan Edwards—developed their theories *well after* the Jesuit scholars of the counter-reformation had formulated alternate interpretations of Bible prophecy. A historical interpretation of the prophecies, to some degree, launched the reformation. The Church of Rome retaliated by introducing a new theory—a fabrication that lingers with us to this day.

Earlier in this book, a number of central beliefs of the two-phase theory were mentioned, but we've only elaborated on a few of them. Let's take a moment to investigate some of these beliefs, and compare them to what the Bible says:

(1) The coming of Christ is *imminent*.

This is the teaching that says that prophecy stopped for 2,000 years between the sixty-ninth and seventieth weeks of Daniel, chapter nine. The Second Coming is considered to be "imminent" because it could happen at any moment, and the reason it could happen at any moment is because there are no prophecies to be fulfilled before He comes. As we have already seen, this is a gross misunderstanding of the 70-week prophecy.

(2) Most of the book of Revelation does not apply to the Christian church today.

It is commonly believed that only the first three chapters of Revelation apply to the Christian church; after that, the church is absent during the seven-year period until the glorious appearing of Christ. We have already seen that there is no mention of a two-phase coming of Christ found anywhere in scripture.

(3) The Holy Spirit, through the Christian church, is the restraining power mentioned in 2 Thessalonians 2:7.

This one is a little more complicated. In Paul's letter, he mentions a power that, in his day, is preventing the appearance of the Antichrist:

For the mystery of lawlessness is already at work; only he who now restrains will do so until he is taken out of the way. And then the lawless one will be revealed, whom the Lord will consume with the breath of His mouth and destroy with the brightness of His coming. (2 Thessalonians 2:7, 8)

It is often assumed that the "restrainer" in this passage is the Holy Spirit through the church. When the church is gone (raptured), the Antichrist is free to make his appearance. Many newer versions of the Bible have capitalized the "he" who does the restraining, assuming that it is in reference to the Holy Spirit.

I imagine that the devil must be chomping at the bit to seize the reigns of planet earth. He has already usurped authority over it by deceiving our first parents, and he implied the world was his to give Jesus during the temptations in the desert. If the devil has a timetable to take over the world, I imagine he believes the sooner the better. There is nothing he would love more than a worldwide kingdom of the Antichrist.

In Paul's letter, is the "restrainer" that keeps the Antichrist in check actually God? Some have argued that Paul was talking about the

Roman Empire, which, according to Daniel 7, would crumble before the appearance of the Antichrist.[31] This interpretation is convincing, but I have to believe that one of the key messages of Bible prophecy is that God is ultimately in control of the destiny of our planet.

Would it be unreasonable, then, to assume that God has taken charge of the time when the Antichrist is allowed to appear? God doesn't have to wait for the church to disappear to allow that to happen, just as God didn't have to remove Job from the planet in order for the devil to do his worst.

The "restrainer" may well be the Holy Spirit—but that doesn't mean the church is absent. To assume this is to read more into the passage than Paul actually writes.

(4) God will not require the church to go through the tribulation.

As we have seen, God has never exempted His people from suffering. In every age, God carries His people through tough times, and provides a promise that He will do so again as earth's history wraps up.

(5) Every time the Bible speaks of Israel, it means the literal nation of Israel.

When you assume that the seventieth week of Daniel's prophecy is something that occurs at the close of history, separated from the rest of the prophecy by two millennia, you are forced to resurrect the literal nation of Israel and press her into service.

There are some problems with this understanding. Think back to the 70-week prophecy again. Gabriel told Daniel explicitly that the time set aside by the prophecy was for his people, the Jews.

When the 70 weeks came to a close in 34 A.D., time was up. There was no mention that the nation of Israel would later be pressed into service again, or that there would be a second probationary period. When the prophecy was complete, so was Israel's tenure in the role that God had previously assigned to her. If this is not the case, then the phrase "seventy weeks are determined for your people" becomes somewhat meaningless.

When you insert a gap of 2,000 years into the prophecy, you're faced with a bit of a problem. How can the last week (or seven years) possibly apply to Israel? To make it work, you have to resurrect the literal nation of Israel.

A Tale of Two Cities

In the books of Daniel and Revelation, two cities are featured prominently—Jerusalem (Daniel's home) and Babylon (Daniel's place of captivity). In Daniel's day, these were in obvious reference to literal cities. When it speaks about the fall of Babylon (chapter 5), it means the literal, historical city of Babylon when the Persian general Cyrus besieged it. When it speaks about the sacking of Jerusalem by the Babylonians, it means the literal city of Jerusalem in Palestine.

In the book of Revelation, however, there's a subtle but significant shift. By the time John is writing this book, the literal city of Babylon had been destroyed, never to be rebuilt again. The 70-week prophecy has come to an end, and the probationary period has closed for the literal city of Jerusalem. What, then, is John referring to?

When you read of these two cities in the book of Revelation, John's reference is not to the ancient, literal cities. Instead, he is using the cities symbolically to point us to something else.

Take, for example, the city of Babylon. It is mentioned six times in the book of Revelation (a very interesting number, by the way—because six is the biblical number of *man*), and each time it is mentioned, it is with reference to manmade religion, religious confusion, and worldly belief systems.[32] These are things that will be destroyed when Christ sets up His kingdom. Jesus will shatter the *spiritual* city of Babylon.

The city of Jerusalem, on the other hand, will prosper as Christ establishes His kingdom. Jerusalem is mentioned only three times in the book of Revelation—once near the beginning, and then twice again near the end.[33] When the subject of Jerusalem is discussed in John's prophecy, there is no mistaking what God is referring to—it is a *heavenly* Jerusalem:

"He who overcomes, I will make him a pillar in the temple of my God, and he shall go out no more. And I will write on him the name of My God and the name of the city of My God, the New Jerusalem, which comes down out of heaven from My God. And I will write on him My new name." (Revelation 3:12)

The language couldn't be clearer. In the book of Revelation, the city of God is the *New* Jerusalem, not the ancient city of the Bible. In the very end, this city comes *down from God out of heaven* (Revelation 21:1-5) and becomes the capital city of a recreated earth.[34]

The apostle John uses the ancient cities of Babylon and Jerusalem as vivid illustrations of an end-time struggle between the forces of Christ and Satan. In Daniel's day, Babylon appeared victorious. God's people were captive in a strange land with strange practices. The temple lay in ruins, and pagan warriors were able to gloat about their victory over the Israelite God. In the end, Babylon collapses as kings from the east invade her (the armies of the Medes and the Persians), and God's plan triumphs over evil.

The story in the book of Revelation is the same; only this time, the whole world is the city of Babylon. God's people are captive in a sinful world, and it seems as if evil is triumphing. The wickedness of the human race continues to grow, and God's people are less and less welcome. In the end, however, a King from the east (Matthew 24:27) flashes across the sky, and the armies of heaven destroy the city of Babylon (Revelation 16:12-21; 19:11-21).

The parallels are so complete that the Euphrates river (which Cyrus dried up so that he could invade Babylon by going under the city walls on the dry river bed—see Isaiah 44:24-45:1) is mentioned, and Cyrus of old is referred to as God's "anointed" (Isaiah 45:1), a term that was usually reserved for the Messiah.

These stories of the Old Testament were handpicked by God to reveal circumstances and attitudes in days just prior to the Second Coming. God's people, once again, will be going back to the city of Jerusalem after long years in captivity—but this time, they'll be going to the *heavenly* Jerusalem.

The re-occupation of literal Israel by the Jews is a little anticlimactic when compared to God's plan for His people, don't you think? What possible purpose would be accomplished by moving everyone back to Palestine and rebuilding the temple? Does God intend to reinstate animal sacrifices?

Not at all. Go back and read the passage from Revelation 3:12 that mentions a heavenly Jerusalem, and you'll notice something very interesting. It also mentions a *temple*. This cannot be a reference to the ancient literal temple in Jerusalem since that was destroyed more than two decades before John wrote these words.

It turns out that God has a *heavenly* temple. The ancient city of Jerusalem foreshadowed the heavenly city of Jerusalem; the ancient temple also foreshadowed a *heavenly* temple—a place where Jesus Christ serves as our High Priest:[35]

Now this is the main point of the things we are saying: We have such a High Priest, who is seated at the right hand of the throne of the Majesty in the heavens, a Minister of the sanctuary and of the true tabernacle which the Lord erected, and not man. (Hebrews 8:1, 2)

The Heavenly Temple is a subject that could occupy hours and hours of Bible study, but for now, it's only important to notice how it forms one of the central themes of the book of Revelation:

*And I said to him, "Sir, you know." So he said to me, "These are the ones who come out of the great tribulation, and washed their robes and made them white in the blood of the Lamb. Therefore they are before the throne of God, and serve Him day and **night in His temple**. And He who sits on the throne will dwell among them." (Revelation 7:14,15, emphasis supplied.)*

*Then **the temple of God** was opened in heaven, **and the ark of His covenant was seen in His temple**. And there were lightnings, noises, thunderings, an earthquake, and great hail. (Revelation 11:19, emphasis supplied.)*

*And I looked, and behold, a white cloud, and on the cloud sat One like the Son of Man, having on His head a golden crown, and in His hand a sharp sickle. And another angel **came out of the temple**, crying with a loud voice to Him who sat on the cloud, "Thrust in Your sickle and reap, for the time has come for You to reap, for the harvest of this earth is ripe." So He who sat on the cloud thrust in His sickle on the earth, and the earth was reaped. Then another angel **came out of the temple which is in heaven**, he also having a sharp sickle. (Revelation 14:14-17, emphasis supplied.)*

*After these things I looked, and behold, **the temple of the tabernacle of the testimony in heaven** was opened. And out of the temple came the seven angels having the seven plagues, **clothed in pure bright linen, and having their chests girded with golden bands**[36]. Then one of the four living creatures gave to the seven angels seven golden bowls full of the wrath of God who lives forever and ever. **The temple** was filled with smoke from the glory of God and from His power, and no one was able to enter **the temple** till the seven plagues of the seven angels were completed. (Revelation 15:5-8, emphasis supplied.)*

The focus of the book of Revelation is not on the literal nation of Israel in Palestine. Rather, it provides a much broader picture. It's a panoramic view of the final moments of a colossal controversy between good and evil. That controversy spans thousands of years and involves the citizens of both earth and heaven. It's the story of how God plans to finally deal with fallen angels and fallen men. The issues are much, much bigger than tanks, planes or guns in the Middle East—and the stakes are much higher than mere political geography.

I have no doubt that God has a special place in His heart for the Jewish people, and there is some indication in the book of Romans that we should expect to see a special work among them before Jesus comes— but when the 490 years of Daniel's 70-week prophecy came to a close, probation for the Jewish nation was over. The restoration of literal Israel and a literal temple in the last days is not part of the prophetic calendar. When Jesus declared the earthly temple to be desolate (Matthew 24:38), He didn't suggest it would only be temporary. He simply said it would be desolate. Personally, I take Him at His word.

The New Testament is abundantly clear that *everyone* can be part of Israel today. All who believe, according to Paul, are considered by God to be descendants of Abraham and a part of the covenants made with him:

For he is not a Jew who is one outwardly, nor is that circumcision which is outward in the flesh; but he is a Jew who is one inwardly, and circumcision is that of the heart, in the Spirit, and not in the letter; whose praise is not from men but from God. (Romans 2:28, 29)

Therefore know that only those who are of faith are sons of Abraham. And the Scripture, forseeing that God would justify the nations by faith, preached the gospel to Abraham beforehand, saying, "In you all the nations shall be blessed." (Galatians 3:7, 8)

Christ redeemed us from the curse of the law, having become a curse for us (for it is written, "Cursed is everyone who hangs on a tree"), that the blessing of Abraham might come upon the Gentiles in Christ Jesus, that we might receive the promise of the Spirit through faith. (Galatians 3:13, 14)

For you are all sons of God through faith in Christ Jesus. For as many of you as were baptized into Christ have put on Christ. There is neither Jew nor Greek, there is neither slave nor free, there is neither male nor female; for you are all one in Christ Jesus. And if you are Christ's, then you are Abraham's seed, and heirs according to the promise. (Galatians 3:26-29)

Notice the fact that Paul specifically refers to all believers as *Israel* when he closes his powerful letter to a church that was apparently struggling with how Gentile and Jewish believers were supposed to coexist:

For in Christ Jesus neither circumcision nor uncircumcision avails anything, but a new creation. And as many as walk according to this rule, peace and mercy be upon them, and upon the Israel of God. (Galatians 6:15, 16)

Today, everyone is faced with a choice. You are either a citizen of spiritual Babylon or you are a citizen of the New Jerusalem. That is the theme of Bible prophecy, and it is a question that will have been decided by the time Jesus appears.

(6) Christ's millennial (thousand-year) reign will be on earth, after the great tribulation.

Really, this is a subject for another book, but I've raised the question for one simple reason: the "secret rapture" theory has everyone transported to heaven for seven years before Christ returns with His church to establish a worldly kingdom.

There is no question that Jesus *does* establish a kingdom on earth. This is evident from the dream that Nebuchadnezzar had—a great stone, representing God's kingdom, demolishes the empires of this world and then grows until it fills the earth. In the book of Revelation we are told, quite plainly, that God will ultimately take up residence with us on this earth:

And I saw a new heaven and a new earth, for the first heaven and the first earth had passed away. Also there was no more sea. Then I, John, saw the holy city, New Jerusalem, coming down out of heaven from God, prepared as a bride adorned for her husband. And I heard a loud voice from heaven saying, "Behold, the tabernacle of God is with men, and He will dwell with them, and they shall be His people, and God Himself will be with them and be their God. (Revelation 21:1-3)

This earthly kingdom, however, doesn't begin the moment Jesus comes for His church. Christ told His disciples that He was going to heaven to prepare a place for them there:

"In My Father's house are many mansions; if it were not so, I would have told you. I go to prepare a place for you. And if I go and prepare a place for you, I will come again and receive you to Myself; that where I am, there you may be also." (John 14:2,3)

We have been promised that we will live in heaven! The two-phase theory says that we will be in heaven during the last seven years of earth's history, but the Bible teaches that our visit to Christ's home will last much, much longer than that.

It is often assumed that the millennial kingdom of Christ (thousand-year kingdom) will be established on this planet, but that theory has overlooked a few key passages of scripture. First of all, when Jesus comes, the wicked will be destroyed at that time. The Bible reveals that the fallen bodies of the wicked become a feast for the birds after the coming of Christ, and that those who are not in Christ at his coming will become food for the eagles. (It is interesting that those who are "taken" are the ones who are destroyed. Read what Jesus says in the second reference very carefully. Popular thinking says that the wicked are "left behind," but the words of Jesus are clear: those who are "taken" are taken as the wicked were in the flood, and the believers are "left behind.") :

Then I saw an angel standing in the sun; and he cried with a loud voice, saying to all the birds that fly in the midst of heaven, "Come and gather together for the supper of the great God, that you may eat the flesh of kings, the flesh of captains, the flesh of mighty men, the flesh of horses and of those who sit on them, and the flesh of all people, free and slave, both small and great." And I saw the beast, the kings of the earth, and their armies, gathered together to make war against Him who sat on the horse and against His army. Then the beast was captured, and with him the false prophet who worked signs in his presence, by which he deceived those who received the mark of the beast and those who worshipped his image. These two were cast alive into the lake of fire burning with brimstone. And the rest were killed with the sword which proceeded from the mouth of Him who sat on the horse. And all the birds were filled with their flesh. (Revelation 19:17-21)

"I tell you, in that night there will be two men in one bed: the one will be taken and the other will be left. Two women will be grinding together: the one will be taken, and the other left. Two men will be in the field: the one will be taken, and the other left." And they answered and said to

Him, "Where, Lord?" So He said to them, "Wherever the body is, there the eagles will be gathered together." (Luke 17:34-37)

The wicked are slain by the coming of Christ, and the righteous are caught up to meet Him in the air, as described in 1 Thessalonians 4:13-17. They are taken, as promised, to be with Jesus in His Father's house—in the place that He has prepared for them. It tells us that Jesus will "bring with Him" those who have fallen asleep, or died. In other words, they will be raised from the dead, and brought with Christ to heaven.

At this point, with the wicked slain and the righteous in heaven, the earth is left *absolutely empty.* It has been broken down by the presence of Christ.[37] Notice this amazing description of the earth during this time in the writings of Jeremiah:

I beheld the earth, and indeed it was without form, and void; and the heavens, they had no light. I beheld the mountains, and indeed they trembled, and all the hills moved back and forth. I beheld, and indeed there was no man, and all the birds of the heavens had fled. I beheld, and indeed the fruitful land was a wilderness, and all its cities were broken down at the presence of the Lord, by His fierce anger. For thus says the Lord: "the whole land shall be desolate; yet I will not make a full end. For this shall the earth mourn, and the heavens above be black, because I have spoken. I have purposed and will not relent, nor will I turn back from it." (Jeremiah 4:23-28)

According to Jeremiah, God's presence breaks down the planet. The mountains and hills, as described in the book of Revelation, have been shaken. The wicked are dead, the righteous are in heaven. The cities are destroyed. The human race is nowhere to be found on the face of the planet. Meanwhile, the saints of God have been taken to heaven to be with Christ:

And I saw thrones, and they sat on them, and judgment was committed to them. And I saw the souls of those who had been beheaded for their witness to Jesus and for the word of God, who had not worshiped the beast or his image, and had not received his mark on their foreheads or on their hands. And they lived and reigned with Christ for a thousand years. But the rest of the dead did not live again until the thousand years were finished.... (Revelation 20:4, 5)

At the end of a thousand years, a period during which the earth is desolate,[38] the New Jerusalem descends to the surface of the earth and

God establishes an earthly kingdom that will last forever. It's a kingdom I know you'll want to be part of:

And I heard a loud voice from heaven saying, "Behold, the tabernacle of God is with men, and He will dwell with them, and they shall be His people, and God Himself will be with them and be their God. And God will wipe away every tear from their eyes; there shall be no more death, nor sorrow, nor crying; and there shall be no more pain, for the former things have passed away." Then He who sat on the throne said, "Behold, I make all things new." And He said to me, "Write, for these words are true and faithful." (Revelation 21:3-5)

(7) Passages of scripture referring to the Second Coming must be divided into two categories: the rapture and the glorious appearing.

We have already looked at this in considerable detail—there is absolutely no indication in the Bible that the writers understood that Christ would come in two phases.

---

[27] In Dave MacPherson, The Incredible Cover-up, p. 49,50

[28] Ibid., p. 60

[29] I must add my thoughts here as well—I, too, am unimpressed with her "gift," for one simple reason. If God were to speak to someone (as is quite possible, according to the New Testament), He would not contradict the clear record of scripture. The Holy Spirit does not contradict Himself. If a two-phase theory is not found in the Bible, Christians are not to be persuaded by the miraculous, for in the last days, even the Antichrist performs "miracles." (See Revelation 13)

[30] Tim LaHaye, et al. Are We Living in the End Times, p. 113

[31] In Daniel 7, we see the same progression of kingdoms as with the statue of Daniel 2, except in a different format. Animals are used to represent nations rather than metals. In Daniel 7, as in Daniel 2, the Roman Empire breaks up into ten pieces—and the Antichrist then appears among those pieces. Thus the Roman Empire would have to crumble before the Antichrist could appear.

[32] See Revelation 14:8; 16:19; 17:5; 18:2, 10, 21

[33] See Revelation 3:12; 22:2, 10

[34] This is in perfect keeping with Paul's assertion that the Christian's citizenship is not on earth, but in heaven. (See Philippians 3:20)

35 You might want to read the eighth and ninth chapters of Hebrews in their entirety—it's quite an eye-opener. The entire temple system of the Old Testament was specifically designed to foreshadow Christ and His work in the Heavenly Sanctuary in our behalf.

36 These are priest-like garments.

37 For descriptions of the destruction of the earth at the return of Christ, See Revelation 6:14-17; Psalm 50:3; 2 Peter 3:10-13

38 With the exception of the devil, who apparently stays here. Revelation 20:1-3 tells us that he is shut up in the "bottomless pit." The original Greek word for this is abussos—the same word used in the Greek Old Testament (Septuagint) to describe the earth when it is "without form and void." The reason that Satan is "bound" during this thousand year period of time is simply because he has nobody to work on—the entire human race is either dead or in heaven.

CHAPTER ELEVEN

Why Jesus is Coming Back

When I was a kid, there was a vent in my bedroom floor that let the heat from a woodstove on the lower level come upstairs. At night, when I was supposed to be sleeping, I would sometimes get out of bed, crawl across the floor and put my ear to the vent. From that position I could hear what my parents were talking about.

You see, I *knew* that if I heard them talking about *me*, I would discover the truth of how they really felt about me. Human nature being what it is, people are more likely to tell the truth when you're not around or when they assume you can't hear them. (Who hasn't had the misfortune of being caught once or twice giving an opinion about someone, only to discover that he or she heard the whole thing?) For the most part, I think my parents liked me—or they knew that I was listening at that vent—because I didn't hear much evidence that they wanted me out of the house.

Now, let me ask you a question: why do you think Jesus is coming back? Two thousand years of Christian history have produced some rather remarkable ideas. While it's true that Christ's return will signal the end of sin and suffering, and it's true that His coming will be accompanied by God's wrath against sin, is that really *why* He's coming?

I believe it's one of the reasons, just not the primary one. It would be hard to respect God if He didn't ultimately deal with sin, or put an end to it. In our hearts, we want a God who will set the record straight. We have an inborn sense of justice that causes us to want Him to make things right. But as important as God's justice is, I don't believe that is the main reason He's coming.

A while ago, as I was reading the seventeenth chapter of John's gospel, a thought occurred to me. In that chapter, Jesus is praying. As you read it, you're actually listening in on an intimate conversation between two members of the Godhead. This prayer is sort of like an open letter to God's children—a conversation He meant for us to hear. It shows us the *mind of God*. He's trying to make Himself known to us.

In a lot of ways, that's what separates Christianity from most of the world's religions. There are belief systems in this world which cause people to punish themselves brutally or to struggle to the brink of insanity attempting to know the minds of their gods. But all the Christian has to do is open the Bible and do a little sanctified eavesdropping. God *wants* us to know Him more intimately; in fact, He invites us to do so:

"But let him who glories glory in this, that he understands and knows Me, that I am the Lord, exercising lovingkindness, judgment, and righteousness in the earth. For in these I delight," says the Lord. (Jeremiah 9:24)

The words written in the Bible allow us to eavesdrop on God—with His permission, of course. And if you eavesdrop on God, you discover the truth about Him. He is loving, fair, and good. You also discover the truth about how He feels about *you*, which takes me back to the seventeenth chapter of John.

In this remarkable passage, God the Son is talking to God the Father about *us*. When you arrive at the twenty-fourth verse, you suddenly make a profound discovery about God that will change your perspective on life forever:

"Father, I desire that they also whom You gave Me may be with Me where I am, that they may behold My glory which You have given Me; for You loved Me before the foundation of the world." (John 17:24)

According to Jesus' own words, it is the *desire* of His heart to be with you. A lot of people I meet seem to feel that the only way God will ever let anyone into heaven is if He is given no choice.

"All right," He says resignedly at the judgment, "I'll let him in, but it's only because I've got no choice. He just barely squeaked by, and I'm going to have to let him in."

The assumption is that God is trying to keep you out while you're struggling to get in; that He'd really rather you didn't come at all, but if you play your cards right, He really won't have much of a choice. He'll have to let you in.

When put in print, it sounds kind of cold—and it is! Yet I'm amazed at how many people have this very picture of God; that our job is to convince Him to let us in.

It makes me wonder why anyone would pursue a relationship with that kind of God at all. It's like a marriage where a husband or wife stays in the relationship for the sake of the children, even though they don't really love their spouse. They grit their teeth and tough it out to the bitter end, suffering unspeakable misery. I sometimes wonder on how many headstones we could write, "She suffered it out to the bitter end."

That is not a real marriage. It is one existing only on paper, and needing a lot of help to become what God intends marriage to be.

Unfortunately, this describes some people's relationship with God. It exists only on paper. They have trouble believing that God *wants* them in a relationship with Him. These people need to carefully read what Jesus said to His Father.

"Father, I *want* them with Me. My will is that they will always be with Me! I want them where I am. I want to take them home."

Specifically, who is Jesus talking about—just the disciples? Could He really be talking about you? A few verses earlier, He makes it clear. Speaking of the disciples, He prays:

I do not pray for these alone, but also for those who will believe in Me through their word. (John 17:20)

As Jesus prays, there is no question that He is thinking about *you*. You are among those who have believed because of the words of the disciples. At that moment, nearly 2,000 years ago, Jesus had *you* in mind. You're the whole reason He's coming back!

He's coming back because He wants you *with Him*. He's coming back because to Him, heaven won't be everything it could be if you're not there. He's coming back because He's got a place for you. "Father," He said, "I want them with Me where I am."

Let not your heart be troubled; you believe in God, believe also in Me. In My Father's house are many mansions; if it were not so, I would have told you. I go to prepare a place for you. And if I go and prepare a

*place for you, I will come again and receive you to Myself; that where I
am, there you may be also. (John 14:1-3)*

So why is it that Jesus is *really* coming back? He's coming back
because He wants you to be with Him. It's as simple as that. You can
complicate it if you want. You can stack all the theology and complex
end-times charts you'd like on top of it, but it all boils down to this; Jesus
wants you there.

It's His fondest wish. It's His deepest desire. He wants nothing more.
I know, because I heard Him say it.

That simple fact has given Christians unspeakable courage throughout
the centuries. That's why Christianity is completely unstoppable. We
know that God *wants* us. This world doesn't want me? No problem.
God does. This world wants me to suffer all kinds of grief and pain?
No problem. I'm going home soon. We can endure just about anything,
because we know it's not forever.

The martyrs, soaked in tar and lit on fire in Nero's arena went willingly,
because they knew it wasn't forever. The early Christians, as they laid
their dead to rest in the catacombs of Rome, knew that resurrection
morning was coming. Their grief was eased by the knowledge that Jesus
wanted them as His friends in the Kingdom of Heaven, and that He
would not forget the dead who died in Him.

The Bible writers allude to the subject of the Second Coming more
than 2,500 times. They spent a lot of time thinking about it because of
the profound realization that, in spite of our imperfections, in spite of our
mistakes, in spite of our sins, *God still wants us.*

Occasionally someone will accuse Christians of being so heavenly
minded that they're of no earthly good. They'll say that we have our
heads in the clouds, that we don't understand reality, and that we do
nothing but think about heaven and the Second Coming.

I suppose that in some instances, the accusations have been true.
Sometimes Christians have a tendency to disconnect from the realities of
the world we live in. We truly *do* need to be of some earthly good—yet
I beg to differ with the critics. In reality, is there anything wrong with
placing all of your hopes in a God who desperately wants you? Is there
really anything wrong with keeping your mind focused on the appearing
of Christ?

When you take a little time to discover for yourself who Jesus is from the pages of the Bible, you can't help but become heavenly minded. Who wouldn't want to be in the presence of someone like Jesus? When you see how desperately He longs for your company, where else could you ever turn? When you see Him hanging limply on a cross, dying under the weight of your sins, and you realize that He could step down from the cross but stays there because He *wants* you, how could you *not* constantly think about His return?

Personally, I'm eager for Jesus to come because I can't wait to meet Him face to face. I have talked with Him for years. I have sat quietly in front of an open Bible and heard His voice. I have sensed His leading in my life. I have spent long hours in meditative prayer with Him. Together, we have built the life I lead, and together, we have laid plans for eternity.

And yet, in spite of the deep personal relationship we've built, I have yet to meet Him face to face. I have come to know Him for who He is, but I have never seen Him. Just like someone becoming acquainted with an Internet bride from a far-off country, I have come to know my suitor through His words to me, but I have yet to set foot in His home. I'm anxious to see Him.

As I read the pages of Scripture, I am certain that He can't wait to see me, either. He prayed for the day that I would finally lay eyes on Him and see the glory of His kingdom. His Book is so full of references to His return that I know it's foremost on His mind. If it seems as if time is dragging by slowly for me as I wait, I get the distinct sense that it must be dragging by slowly for Him, too. He delays His coming to be certain that all those who can be saved for the kingdom will be saved. (See 2 Peter 3:9.)

But heaven will not wait forever. The waiting will be over before we know it.

I will never forget one morning when my wife came up the stairs of our little house to find me. She had a funny look on her face, and I knew that she was wrestling to find the right words with which to give me the news. It was obviously going to be an announcement of some importance. In reality, she didn't *have* to say anything. I could pretty much guess what it was just from looking at her face.

I swallowed hard, scarcely daring to say the words: "You're *pregnant*, aren't you?"

She started to laugh and cry all at the same time, which was her way of saying "yes".

From that moment on, I don't think I have ever seen Jean work as hard as she did to get ready for that baby. When she found out she was going to be a mother, her energy level shot through the roof—and she just about killed us both.

I was dragged to every baby convention, baby shop, baby shower, baby fair, baby class, baby lecture, and baby superstore in the city. I had no idea that babies were responsible for so much of the world's economy!

In addition, we had to paint the baby's room, buy the baby's furniture, get the baby's clothes, pick out a baby car seat, and read just about every child-rearing book or magazine ever published. My wife, bless her heart, was trying to make me an expert on babies. It was a futile effort, because a couple of children later, I still don't know anything about babies. In fact, I'm more confused than ever.

Getting ready was very important to Jean. We travel a lot, and because of that she knew time would slip away all the more quickly. She didn't want to be caught unprepared.

There were a lot of things I worried about. How were we going to make ends meet? What if I wasn't a good father? What did I know about child rearing, anyway?

There was one thing, however, I didn't worry about. I wasn't the slightest bit worried about the time the baby would arrive. Of all the information I read in the baby books, I had picked up on one essential piece of information. Your first baby will always arrive late. The book told me so.

Our due date was November 3. When the day drew near, we were across the country from our home, holding a series of evangelistic meetings. About half way through the meetings my wife flew home, because the airlines don't like it if expectant mothers fly too close to their due date. I suppose they're afraid that drastic elevation changes will induce labor, and they don't like having to deliver a baby in the back of a passenger jet.

By the time Jean left, I think she was technically past the final date that airlines no longer want pregnant women to fly, but I wasn't worried, because I knew what the book said; your first child will come late. There was no way our baby was going to try to make its entrance into the world while Jean was in the air.

I also knew that I would be home in plenty of time to witness the birth of our first child. I was scheduled to arrive home more than a week ahead of the due date and, allowing for the fact that your first child always comes late, I would be there at least two weeks ahead of the big event.

There was only one hitch. Our baby forgot to read the book. She came two weeks early.

When Jean first went into labor, she tried to call me, but there was no answer. The reason? I had taken the phone off the hook the night before so I could get a little well-deserved sleep. We had been working unusually long hours, and I hoped to sleep in until at least seven o'clock in the morning. The only way I could guarantee an interruption-free night was to disconnect the phones for a little while. It never occurred to me that the baby might choose to come early.

When I got up the next morning, I turned the phone back on. It started ringing immediately. It was Don, a friend of mine, and the local pastor.

"Shawn," he said, "I have two pieces of news for you. First of all, we've got a Bible worker coming to help us with all of the new people that are coming to church. She'll be here tomorrow."

That was fantastic news. We were so busy with new converts that we needed all the help we could get.

"That's great! What's the second bit of news, Don?"

"Well, you might want to phone your wife, because I think you're about to become a father."

My stomach tightened. A cold sweat broke out on my forehead. I was sure I would now be sleeping on the couch for the rest of my married life. I immediately phoned home, but of course, Jean was no longer there. Panicking, I called directory assistance and got the number for the hospital. When I called in, they patched me through to the labor room. I asked the nurse if I could speak to my wife.

Let me pause for a moment and share some hard-earned advice. I can't think of a worse moment to ask your wife to come to the phone than when she's in labor. It was not a good idea.

"Hi, honey!" I said with all the courage I could muster. "How are you?"

My wife spoke a couple of words—I can't bring them to mind—and then she hung up on me.

I called back. The nurses told me that if I moved quickly, I might actually make it home before the baby arrived. It was a little gleam of light at the end of a very dark tunnel. I quickly called the airline to see if I could get a flight. I could, but I paid a premium for it. In about 7 hours I would be home.

Scrambling to throw a few things into a suitcase, I raced for the airport. Once the plane was airborne, I rushed to the washroom to take a look at myself. I still hadn't shaved. I knew if I arrived at my child's birth looking scruffy, I would never live it down. I dashed back out into the main cabin and flagged down a flight attendant.

"Listen," I said, "you've got to help me. My wife is in the hospital giving birth to our first child, and I need to look decent when I get there. Do you have a razor?"

I could only hope for the impossible. Was it possible that they had a few grooming kits on board from some international flight?

"Let me look," she said. All of the flight attendants put their heads together to see what they could come up with. One of them dipped into her own suitcase and pulled out a razor she had already used on her legs. "It's all I've got," she said, "and I know it's used, but we can sterilize it."

Sterilize it—at 30,000 feet? She disappeared into the galley, swished the razor in a glass of vodka, and then handed it to me, beaming. I ran back to the washroom to shave. That dull razor gave me the worst shave of my life.

At last feeling somewhat presentable, I ran back to my seat and called the hospital again from one of those $10-a-minute phones in the back of the seat. To my surprise, this time Jean answered the phone herself. Her voice was as sweet as ever.

"Oh, hi honey! Would you like to know what we had?"

It was all over—sooner than I thought.

Six hours later, I was holding my little girl in my arms for the first time. Every parent knows how it feels. All the work, the worrying, and the scrambling to get ready was now over.

We had known for months a child was coming. We had read about it, we had dreamed about it, and we had prepared for it. The miracle of ultrasound had given us a tiny glimpse of our child; we were able to hear the heartbeat and feel the occasional kick. But until this moment, we had not yet met our child face-to-face. That event came sooner than we expected.

One of the most wonderful days of our married life came when we carried our little girl over the threshold of our house and placed her in the nursery. We didn't take her into our home grudgingly. We didn't let her in because the law said we had to take her home and feed her. We *wanted* her there. We had prepared for the event.

Jesus tells us that He has gone to prepare a place for us. In such an hour as we think not, He's going to come back. It will be over much sooner than we think.

In Matthew 24, Jesus gives us signs to watch for. He compares them to the contractions of labor pain. As the pace of world events gathers speed, the Second Coming draws closer and closer. We watch and wait expectantly for indications that it's just about time. One of my favorite Christian authors put it well when she said, "the last movements will be rapid ones."

Jesus watches the signs just as impatiently, I believe, because He's anxious to take us home. He's eager for a reunion. All of heaven is ablaze with activity, getting our places ready. They know that time is running out.

Right now, they're putting the finishing touches on our mansions. The banquet table is being set. The place cards are being put out. Is there one with your name? There's a choir practice tonight for the biggest celebration in the history of the universe. Then, the angels look over the books one last time to make sure everything is in order.

Is your name there in heaven's books?

You know, sometimes when you eavesdrop you hear things you don't want to hear. Sometimes you discover what people really think of you, and it's devastating. But when you eavesdrop on God, that won't ever happen. He knows the truth about your life, and He still wants you.

"Father," said Jesus, "I want them. I want to take them home with Me."

As this tired old world starts to fall apart, does your heart long for something better? Do you have a sense that this world is not really your home? In your heart, is there a distant memory of Eden and a distinct sense that life was not supposed to be lived the way we live it now?

Life in this world can be very disappointing. That's why it's important to remember that this place is not our home.

The story is told of a missionary and his wife who became very ill from adverse living conditions and overwork. Eventually, the missionary board called them back home. They didn't really want to return, but his health became so fragile that they knew they had no choice.

Reluctantly, they boarded a ship for North America. Before long, they discovered that one of their shipmates was a retiring diplomat also heading home. They discovered this man to be a filthy lecher who got drunk every night and used four-lettered words in every conversation. Even though obviously married, He made passes at all the girls on the ship. He was so rude and obnoxious that it didn't take long until most of the people on board were wishing the journey were over so they could be rid of him.

When the ship finally steamed into port, there was a large band of people on the dock waiting to meet the ship. It was a welcoming party for the diplomat. As he made his way down the gangplank, a marching band started to play. The newspaper was present and took his picture as he was awarded a gold plaque for all his years of service. The diplomat's wife received a massive bouquet of roses. The whole crowd cheered.

It was a different story, however, when the missionary and his wife made their way down the ramp. Nobody noticed them. In fact, most of the crowd had moved on to follow the diplomat to his retirement party. The missionaries had to carry their own suitcases and flag down a taxi to take them to an inexpensive motel for the night.

As they stood on the curb waiting for a taxi, the missionary heard subdued sniffles and noticed that his wife was crying. "What's the matter, honey?" he asked.

"It's not fair," she said. "That indecent man got a party and a plaque and we got nothing at all! Our health is ruined, we haven't got a penny to our name, and nobody even came to meet us!"

Moved with compassion, he slipped his arm around her. "But honey," he said, "We're not home yet."

You and I are not home yet. This world carries huge disappointments for the Christian. But it won't be long now. Soon, we'll be home. Jesus will appear:

Then the King will say to those on his right hand, "Come, you blessed of My Father, inherit the kingdom prepared for you from the foundation of the world. (Matthew 25:34)

It won't be long now. I know, because I "overheard" an important conversation the other day. Jesus *longs* for it to happen. Are you ready?

*Come, you blessed of My Father, inherit the kingdom
prepared for you from the foundation of the world.*

A P P E N D I X   O N E

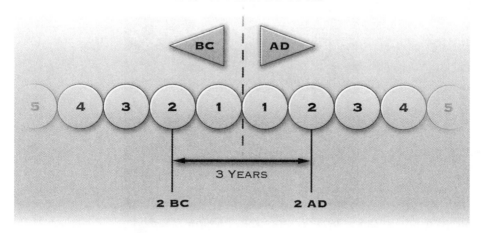

CROSSING FROM BC TO AD

If the above diagram were a number line, the numbers on the left of the dotted line would be negative numbers and the numbers on the right would be positive numbers. Usually, negative two plus three would equal positive one—but on a date line, you get a different result. There is no year zero, so 1 B.C. was immediately followed by the year 1 A.D. Therefore, if you start in 2 B.C. and add three years, you get 2 A.D. (Start in 2 B.C., count three years to the right, and you'll arrive at 2 A.D.). The easiest way to perform this calculation is to simply add one year to your result when you cross the B.C./A.D. line.

Additional copies of this book are available
from It Is Written.
For more information call toll free:
1-888-664-5573
or visit:
www.itiswritten.com

BIBLIOGRAPHY

_____. A Brief History of the Apocalypse.
[Online] Available at http://www.abhota.info/end1.htm,
February 14, 2005.

_____. The Dresden Codex.
[Online] Available at http://www.tu-dresden.de/slub/proj/maya/mayaeng.html,
February 14, 2005.

Asimov, Isaac. Book of Facts. New York: Wing Books, 1979.

Baruffa, Antonio. The Catacombs of St. Callixtus. Vatican City:
Libreria Editrice Vaticana, 2000.

Canadian Press. Allied Bombing of Dresden symbol of war's horror;
60th anniversary nears. [Online] Available at http://www.mytelus.com/news/
article.do?pageID=cp_travel_home&articleID=1840821,
February 14, 2005

Feyerabend, Henry. So Many Religions: Why? Oshawa: Maracle Press, 1994.

Forbush, William (Ed.). Fox's Book of Martyrs. Chicago:
John C. Winston Company, 1926.

Josephus, Flavius. Complete Works of Josephus. Grand Rapids:
Kregel Publications, 1981.

Ladd, George Eldon. The Blessed Hope. Grand Rapids:
Wm. B. Eerdmans Publishing Co., 1978.

LaHaye, Tim and Jenkins, Jerry. Are We Living in the End Times? Wheaton:
Tyndale House, 1999.

LaHaye, Tim and Hindson, Ed. The Popular Encyclopedia of Bible Prophecy.
Eugene, Oregon: Harvest House Publishers, 2004.

Lindsey, Hal. The Late Great Planet Earth. Grand Rapids: Zondervan, 1977.

MacPherson, Dave. The Incredible Cover-up. Medford, Oregon:
Omega Publications, 1980

Nova, Bioterror. PBS Airdate: February 12, 2002.

Penton, M. James. Apocalypse Delayed. Toronto: University of Toronto Press, 1985.

Radice, Betty (Ed.) Herodotus: The Histories. New York: Penguin Books, 1972.

Stratos, Anita. Perchance to Dream.
[Online] Available http:// www.touregypt.net/featurestories/dream.htm
February 13, 2005

Discover More

If you've been blessed by the message
of this book, you'll also enjoy additional
books and materials authored by Shawn
Boonstra and available from It Is Written.
Visit our website at: www.itiswritten.com
and discover a host of spiritual resources
including: music videos, DVDs, cassettes
and CDs, seminar materials, dynamic
presentation graphics, Bible study guides,
audio sermons and much more.

www.itiswritten.com

Free Bible Guides

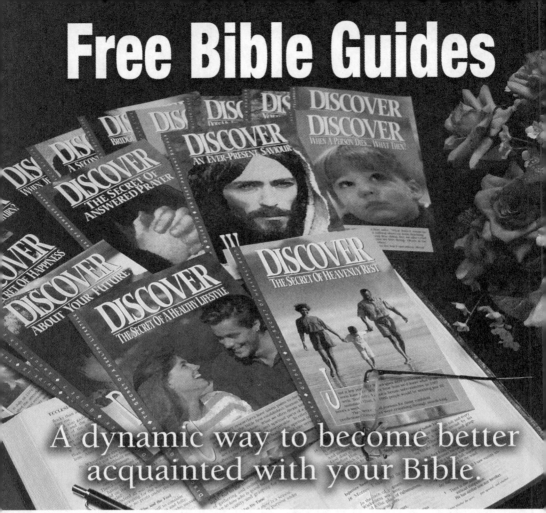

A dynamic way to become better acquainted with your Bible.

The DISCOVER BIBLE GUIDES are designed for busy people like you. They will help bring your Bible to life and you can study at home at your own pace. No cost or obligation. Simply mail the coupon below, or call now to begin a new adventure with your Bible. The DISCOVER BIBLE GUIDES are also available online.

IT IS WRITTEN

CALL TODAY
1-800-253-3000
OR LOG ONTO:
www.itiswritten.com

❏ **YES**, please send me the **FREE *Discover Bible Guides*.**

Name _____ Phone _____

Address _____

City _____ State _____ Zip _____

Please mail this coupon to: **It Is Written, Box O, Thousand Oaks, CA 91359**

Discover Anwers
to life's
Questions

Bibleinfo.com offers answers to hundreds of everyday questions. Discover what the Bible has to say about your question. The answer is only a click away!

KidsBibleinfo.com™
big answers for little people℠

Plus, there is a fun, educational and inspirational site designed for children. Explore interactive games, Bible lessons, character-building stories and more at www.KidsBibleinfo.com.

Bibleinfo.com®

Bible answers to hundreds of life's questions in 17 languages.